LIFE
SUCCESS
HACKS

How to Use Simple Action
to Achieve Anything
You Imagine

LIFE
SUCCESS
HACKS

How to Use Simple Action
to Achieve Anything
You Imagine

Derian B. Tuitt

Life Success Hacks

ISBN-13: 978-0-9988546-9-4
ISBN-10: 0-9988546-9-7

Published by: Celebrity Expert Author
http://celebrityexpertauthor.com

Canadian Address:
1108 - 1155 The High Street
Coquitlam, BC Canada
V3B 7W4
Phone: (604) 941-3041
Fax: (604) 944-7993

US Address:
1300 Boblett Street
Unit A-218
Blaine, WA 98230
Phone: (866) 492-6623
Fax: (250) 493-6603

For my grandfather, Edward "Eddie" Benjamin.

*I remember always being at your side as a very young boy,
up until my mid-twenties when you departed this realm.
Your wisdom continues to have a profound impact on my life.
Thank you!*

TABLE OF CONTENTS

Foreword

I IMAGINE MOST people can remember the day they met Derian Tuitt. He's not the kind of guy you can easily forget. I remember when he introduced himself to me at a speaker event I was hosting, MoMondays. With absolute clarity and conviction, he told me exactly what he wanted and what he was willing to do to make it happen. That is very rare, and very memorable. He told me he wanted to become a professional speaker and within weeks he was doing it. He takes massive action and inspires people along the way.

This book is a blueprint for success and reading it feels like you are sitting down for a conversation with Derian where you leave inspired, energized and feeling unstoppable.

Derian is a living example of what is possible when you take action and trust the process. This book will inspire you to become a better person and give you practical tips on how to do it.

My advice to you is to read this book cover to cover and take lots of notes. The author has lived experiences that you and I can only dream of, and some experiences we would never wish on anyone. From remorse, guilt, shame, and forgiveness to living with passion, purpose, and dignity, Derian shares his wisdom powerfully on these pages.

Do the exercises, commit to taking action, and success will be yours!

Majeed Mogharreban
Founder of The Expert Speaker Institute

Preface

THE IDEA TO write this book was born from my desire for a manual that my daughter can reference while achieving her goals and dreams. In the process of writing, however, I thought about the less than one percent of people who are ready to take serious action to go after their dreams, and who embody the willingness to undergo the personal transformation that is absolutely necessary in order to achieve success. Thus, the book has evolved into what it is today.

Because I took action, I was able to overcome poverty and become:

- A Top Soccer Player

- A Successful Real Estate Investor

- A Certified Professional Accountant

- A Published Author

- A Certified Expert Speaker

Whatever you hold true as your dream or goal, by taking action, you will accomplish it.

Introduction

MOST BOOKS ON achieving success and going after your dreams are filled with nice-sounding and new-age buzz words. The word *manifestation* quickly comes to mind. These books portray success as if it were a destination rather than a journey. They make it seem like a person will just arrive *there* once they recite a few affirmations and the like. People gravitate to this approach because, from what I have noticed, they are in love with the destination, but not so much with the required action it takes to get there. As such, a wake-up call is in effect, provided within the pages of this book in your hands.

Page by page, this book cuts through all the fancy buzz words and lets you know what it is all about: putting in the work. It is time to become a person of action. Plain and Simple! That is how goals and dreams come true. At times, you will have to do things outside of your comfort zone. This is all a part of the process. Otherwise, success – whatever it means to you – will continue to elude you, until you realize that the ultimate life success hack is to take action – now.

This book will highlight actions that you get to do when starting your journey towards your goals and dreams, and it will also let you in on some concepts that will aid you on your mission. Concepts that other success books either fail to mention, or only casually touch on. With all that said, of course no approach is without its pitfalls. This book will identify said pitfalls and provide practical solutions to help you along the way. And yes, I am aware that we all have different goals and dreams, and that success means different things to different people. I get all of that. But no matter what your desires are, you will still be required to take action if you hope to have them manifested in your life. See what I did there?

Now allow me to be extremely honest and direct. This book is not for everyone, nor was it written for everyone. This might be the only time you hear an author making such a revelation that his or her book was not written for everyone, but it is a fact that those who really need to get a copy will not bother to do so. And that is okay. The important thing is that you are here, now. The reality is that your success is your decision and your responsibility. No one is coming to save you. This book will help you get started. Time to take action!

There is no passion to be found in playing small – in settling for a life that is less than the one you are capable of living.

~ Nelson Mandela

SECTION ONE

The Tools

Chapter 1

Trust & Faith: The Wonder Twins

Seek always for the answers within. Do not be influenced by those around you – by their thoughts or their words.

~ Eileen Caddy

WARNING! THIS CHAPTER will either make you uncomfortable or it may inspire you. It is going to mess with some hardcore beliefs you have around this twin subject. And for this, I do not apologize. We all hear the same misleading statements such as, "You cannot trust strangers" or "Trust in God, but not in Man" and how about everyone's favourite mantra, "Trust is difficult to build, but easily broken"?

And these are just those myths that pertain to relationships with other people. As for trusting ourselves, this is an entirely different drama, as we are extremely deficient when it comes to trusting ourselves. We often lack the faith and belief that we can do more than what we are currently doing, thus we eventually settle for security.

Let me tell you this: If you desire success of any kind, you will have to trust and have faith in yourself. Let me also get this out of the way. You cannot do IT alone. So, you need to trust others as well. If you do not grasp this fact you might as well forget about living the life you truly want. Full stop! Trusting is akin to having faith. They are synonymous when you really think about it. You can't have one without the other. Your faith has to be unwavering and unflinching. You have to trust that each step you take is the correct one for you, right now.

Hold on A Sec

I know! I know! The daily newscasts bombard you with stories about dishonest people who cheat others out of their life savings, and more. And these incidents scare the crap out of you. I get it. But please change the channel. You were not placed on Earth to be consumed with negativity. At one time in my life, I had yet to change that channel, but I knew I wanted more out of life for me and my family. That is when I put the Wonder Twins into action. Here is how it all went down.

Because of circumstances in my early childhood, I always dreamed of achieving financial success. However, I did not have the foggiest idea of what to do. All I knew was that I wanted something that would afford me the lifestyle that I craved. How would I figure out the action to make this happen? I remembered what my friend told me: "When in doubt, go to the gym, go for a walk..." One day something happened at the gym during one of my very early morning workouts.

For a few weeks, I had been noticing how a particular individual was always in a great mood. He appeared to have no stresses or worries in the world, especially those of the financial kind. He had a permanent smile on his face and seemed really happy and contented. He came across to me as someone who was free... financially free, worry free, stress free and living his dream. *I wanted that!*

You see, I grew up in extremely difficult conditions. There was no money for basic necessities, much less for luxuries. It seemed as though we were always dependent on someone else for our survival, whether it be the government, the church, whoever or whatever. Over time, once I was able to escape these tough situations, I got a great education and entered the corporate world.

Before long, I was spending my days doing unsatisfying tasks, spinning my wheels to pay the bills; feeling as though I was compromising myself along the way. Do you know the feeling? How it feels to be at the same place each day, where other people are telling you what to do, what to say, how to do and say it, as well as a host of other undesirable experiences?

I find it troubling, being compelled to be at a certain place, doing a certain task for a certain number of hours every week, for roughly forty years. Ouch! I wanted to experience something different. I wanted to spend my time doing all the things that I loved doing. In one word, I wanted FREEDOM, the same as this guy at the gym was clearly experiencing.

So, I approached him and asked point blank what he did for a living, and said that whatever it was, that he needed to teach me. Just telling me was not enough... No! No! No! He had to teach me, as well.

Of course, I knew this was a strange request on my part. So, I told him the reason, that I wanted to be like him. That is, smiling all the time, full of joy, having the freedom to do whatever it is I want to do at any particular time; doing things because I wanted to do them and not because I *had* to do them (yes, there is a huge difference).

I guess he was either impressed with my unique approach or felt I was a sucker because he invited me to meet him for coffee later that day. During our meeting he advised me that real estate was his business and that he owned a lot of properties. He had my attention. He was very brief, so I then asked him about ways in which I could kick-start the process for myself. He mentioned that the easiest way to get started is to partner up with someone who already had a system. And, of course, he *happened* to have such a system.

Here is the nerve-racking part. To get into his system, the minimum I could invest was $200K. Remember, I had never spoken to the guy prior to that day. I did not know him. And as we would say in the Caribbean, "I did not know his parents either." Not sure why knowing the parents part was important, but you get the gist.

Worst of all, I did not have two hundred thousand dollars. As a matter of fact, I was in debt. He must have known what I was thinking because he then mentioned that one must be willing to trust in order to be successful: trust others, as well as trust myself. In other words, he was implying that I should have faith in myself and in him.

A Life-Changing Decision

I had all the reasons to run and run fast: meeting someone for the first time who mentions the subject of money, tells me the minimum amount to invest, and suggests I bring said money to him. It was the perfect scenario for doubt and skepticism to raise their heads. Instead, the Wonder Twins of faith and trust sprung into effect. I made the decision then and there that I was willing to do whatever it takes to achieve my dream of financial freedom. I was going to do whatever it was that this gentleman suggested I do.

I trusted that my gut feeling about this person was correct, that he was a good guy. I had faith that I would be able to come up with two hundred thousand dollars within twelve months (that is what I promised him) and that all will be well in the end.

I was excited and ready to get started, whatever that meant. However, there was one remaining humungous obstacle. I had to get my wife on board. Good luck with that! Convincing her to do something she is not comfortable with is like getting a man to ask for directions when he is lost. It rarely happens.

Time to Face My Spouse

Anyway, all giddy and excited, I told her that evening that I had met someone. Take it from me. Never begin a sentence with those words to your spouse. When I realized that she was getting the wrong idea, I mentioned that it was not another female, but a guy. Double whammy. So, I stopped, took a deep breath, and started again. I told her about my conversation with this gentleman and of my decision to proceed as advised. She immediately shot it down. Imagine a skeet shooter at the Olympics. She could not support my decision. She had concerns. Who was this guy? The fact that he mentioned money must mean that he is a scam artist. On and on she went.

All this time, I just sat there, smiling. My gut was telling me that I am doing the right thing – for me. I politely interrupted her (is there such a thing as politely interrupting someone?) and said,

"Darling, it is okay if you are not on board. Let us separate while we are still friends." I was going to take action with or without her. I was not going to let anyone or anything stand in my way of taking action. But, why was I willing to risk my marriage? Why was I willing to trust this guy who I had only spoken to for the first time that day? What was it that enabled me to make such a determined decision and take an even more drastic stand?

To put it bluntly, I was sick and tired of being sick and tired and I wanted things to change. I was sick of being afraid of failure. And worse, I was sick of feeling insignificant. So, I decided to go all in. Was I scared? Hell, yeah. I was terrified with all capitals: TERRIFIED. Still, I was going to trust and have faith in both myself and this person I had just met. Let's do this!

At this point, when I proposed the idea of separating, my wife said to me to give her some more time to think about it. I figured she needed between two weeks to a month to wrap her head around it, so I agreed to give her the time to mull things over. However, literally about two minutes later, she told me she had an answer. She was on board. Little did I know that I was utilizing one of the Universe's Laws.

The moment you begin trusting and having faith in yourself is the moment others start trusting and having faith in you. People feel toward you how you feel toward yourself. In other words, they only believe in you when you believe in yourself. In any event, it was a great feeling to have my wife's support because, quite frankly, it would have been extremely difficult without her.

Getting her on board was supposed to be the hardest part, and that challenge was overcome on the first day. Momentum was on my side. Now it was time to come up with the $200K. I needed some sort of motivation so I decided that I would not return to the gym until I came up with the money to invest. That, and the fact that the gentleman was going to be at the gym, and I did not want to have to face him for fear that he would think I was just a talker. It did not dawn on me that I could have simply gone to the gym at another time of the day. Nor did I consider that I had agreed to have the money in one year, rather than one day. Those little details got lost in the fray of my mind in motion.

Action Time

Over the next few months, my wife and I set out on the goal of obtaining $200K. The banks turned us down a few times. I kept going back. Faith was at work. I *knew* that we would have a breakthrough. I was not going to take no for an answer.

The months went on and a year's time was drawing nearer, when one day, something happened. To spare you the details, one bank decided to lend us fifty thousand dollars. That is when I got the idea to visit four other banks in a 48-hour period. I trusted my intuition and within the 48-hour time frame, we were able to obtain another $290K, bringing the grand total to $340K. It was at this point that I realized it took us less than the year deadline to which I had agreed. It took nine months and I was able to get an extra $140K to boot. Yes!

Finally! I could now go back to the gym. For months, I had been freaking out that I might get a big stomach from my lack of working out. I was in disbelief at what my wife and I were able to accomplish. Excited! In shock at the same time.

Anyway, I called the gentleman and told him that we had the funds. Now if you think trusting and having faith were required to get my wife's support and to raise the $200K, it was nothing in comparison to giving a total stranger a cheque for 340 thousand dollars. While I was sweating bullets, I kept a cool disposition. My brain was asking me questions such as "Dude, are you insane?" and "What is wrong with you?" and "Are you trying to commit suicide?" My mental state was in total chaos, meanwhile, for some reason, I was at ease in my core.

I equated that to meaning that Infinite Intelligence or God (or whatever we choose to call the great force) was letting me know that the Universe had my back. Things were going to be okay. All I had to do was trust and have faith. And so, I decided to rely on the Wonder Twins to help me through the doubt-filled and nerve-racking times. Have faith that all will be well.

As for the mistaken beliefs that had been passed on to me pertaining to the issue of trust, the following is an example of how I went about debunking my belief system.

Myth: You cannot trust strangers

My wife was a stranger to me before we met. I was a stranger to my friends before we got to know each other. Get the point? We are all strangers at one stage or another. I find it amazing how little trust and faith we have in each other as human beings.

Listen, I am not saying that you should have a cavalier attitude by going around telling random people your entire life story or giving them two hundred thousand dollars. If you do not have a warm feeling about someone when you meet, then do what is right for you.

However, bear in mind that what we think becomes our reality. So, when we already believe someone is untrustworthy, this creates that situation, and prevents us from truly living in harmony as a species. To live a super-fantabulous life, trust and faith are required.

Myth: Trust in God, but not in Man

Growing up in the Caribbean, I used to hear this myth all the time. So, I got to thinking. Those who regurgitate or spew this nonsense are the same ones who will tell you that God lives inside of human beings. It seems to me that if God lives in Man, and we should trust God, then by default we are able to trust Man. And if this is not so, are you willing to go on record by saying Man is more powerful than God when it comes to who is in control? In his book, *The Law of Success in Sixteen Lessons,* Napoleon Hill had this to say: "Trust men and they will be true to you; trust them greatly and they will show themselves great." Think about that.

Myth: Trust is difficult to build, easily broken

This is junk. Trusting someone is a choice, no matter how often they let us down. Too often, we blame someone else for breaking the bond of trust. It is our choice as to whether the bond is broken or not. To illustrate, let me share a story that was told to me by a friend of mine. His name is Milton.

When Milton was a young boy, his father gave him a dollar bill and put him in charge of securing the bank note. Milton placed the dollar in his pocket. When his dad asked him for it about an hour later, Milton realized that he had misplaced the money. With his dad's help, he was able to find the dollar and he returned it to his dad. Milton begged his dad to give the dollar to him again. He promised to secure the money this time. However, being absent-minded, Milton tore the dollar into several pieces.

Again, his dad asked him for the money. Again, there was an issue. Receiving the scraps, his dad taped the dollar together, at which time Milton pleaded again for his dad to give him the dollar. Twice his dad had trusted him with securing the money. Twice Milton had done otherwise. Yet his dad gave him the dollar again. And what did Milton do? He kept the money safe. He had learned.

The point of the story is that Milton's dad trusted him, even after he had messed up twice. His dad made a choice. Each time, he wiped the slate clean of his son's transgression. Also, Milton trusted and had faith in himself that he could carry out his father's request, even after failing the first two times.

I know what you are thinking. *But that story was about a small boy and not much was at stake.* Oh yeah? Tell that to Milton, who professed that the lesson learned from his dad's faith and trust in him enabled him to be the responsible man he is today.

Milton is now 80 years old and is very successful.

Listen, I am not in any way suggesting that you should allow someone to take advantage of your trust in them. If they betray you and you cannot wipe the slate clean, then terminate the relationship, whether it be business or personal.

So, are you uncomfortable as yet? Or are you now inspired? Maybe a bit of both? Faith and trust are two sides of the same coin. Summon them together to work for you. You will be amazed at the transformation in your life when you utilize the power of these Wonder Twins.

Faith is the only true law of success.

~ Ralph Waldo Trine

Chapter 2

Focus: The Game-Changer

One reason so few of us achieve what we truly want is that we never direct our focus; we never concentrate our power.

~ Tony Robbins

IN TODAY'S FAST-PACED society, many people struggle with doing the things necessary to bring about radical and rewarding change in their lives. Being focused is extremely vital and important for success in any endeavour. As stated by John C. Maxwell, author of *Thinking for a Change,* "The only way to get to the next level is to focus, as this practice can bring energy and power to almost anything, whether physical or mental."

First, figure out your goal or dream; it will be the one thing that you want more than anything else. You should be *obsessed* – yes, you read that correctly – with achieving what it is you imagine.

So, for example, you would like to earn more money. You may want to get in shape, perhaps shedding a few pounds or building more muscle mass. You may want to become a physicist.

It does not matter what it is you want to be, do, or have in your life. Here is the point. Focus a laser beam on performing the activities that will enable you to achieve your goal. Select a plan of action and stick with it. The longer you focus your mind on a particular desire, ways and means for its realization begin to come into your consciousness. The solution to any potential problem will also come to you. All that is left for you to do is to act on them. Yes, I will keep reminding you.

Sounds simple, huh? The problem is that we do not stay with anything long enough to see its fruition. In the case of getting in shape, we may jump from diet to diet or from workout to workout, instead of staying the course with one plan or program.

The same applies to wanting to make more money. We jump from one opportunity to another, working on several different projects, and whenever a new and exciting idea comes along, we jump on that one too. This is akin to a farmer planting a seed of a certain crop today, and tomorrow, plucking it out of the ground and planting a seed of a different crop. I think you can agree with me that if he keeps doing this, he will end up with a barren land and his family will starve.

The great author, Harry A. Overstreet, remarked: "The immature mind hops from one thing to another; the mature mind seeks to follow through." In order for results to germinate, one has to apply focus to what one is doing and not become enticed by every wind that blows by. Thomas Fuller, Chaplain to Charles II of England exclaimed, "He that is everywhere is nowhere."

Distraction is the order of the day for us. What we fail to realize is that a focused mindset gives a person immediate confidence. People with a focused mindset do not allow themselves to be distracted or side-tracked. We must be vigilant in order to attain success.

Now we come to the silent enemy. Silent because most people think it is a virtue, when in fact, it is a vice when working to achieve your goal. This kryptonite is called **multi-tasking**. Multi-tasking dilutes your power and, for this reason, top performers and high achievers avoid this practice at all cost.

Multi-tasking adds distractions and mental clutter, resulting in one not being able to concentrate or think with clarity. On the other hand, focused thinking enables solutions to potential problems. No one achieves greatness by multi-tasking. You will not perfect a skill by diluting your attention to its development.

If you are not convinced as yet by the power of focus, consider these two pieces of evidence. First, let us consider the Sun. The Sun is a powerful force of energy that provides warmth to the Earth. However, take a magnifying glass and focus on a particular area, and with the power of the Sun's rays, before long, a potentially deadly fire is quickly created.

Let us also take a look at a laser beam. A laser is a much, much, weaker source of energy than the Sun. When focused, however, it can drill a hole in a diamond or wipe out cancerous cells.

The concept of focus is a life success hack in any endeavour. Spreading your thoughts over multiple subjects and in so many directions will lead to indecision and weakness. Here are a few suggestions to help you with the process of focusing:

1.   *Choose a Chief Aim*

To reiterate, find the one thing that you would like to become, or do, or have. In other words, find out what you are passionate about. Then focus on your strong desire for the attainment of what you imagine. How can you tell if you have a strong desire?

It must be something that consumes you. For you, the success or failure of achieving or becoming that thing is a matter of life and death. I know this is a strong way to describe it. Creating change in your life is not for the faint of heart. Only those with strong dispositions are willing to go through the process of making meaningful, rewarding changes in their lives.

2. *Set Goals*

A plan of action is necessary in order to achieve your chief aim. You now need to set goals. The purpose of goals is to provide direction. The mind will not focus until it has clear objectives. People with goals succeed because they know where they are going. How can you get to your destination if you have not charted a course?

To illustrate, imagine a ship about to leave a port. The captain is navigating the ship toward a definite goal. Now let us look at another ship. It has no goal. Worse, there is no captain at the helm. Even with the engine started, chances are the ship will not get out of the harbour. If it does, it will either sink or end up somewhere on a shore, all smashed to pieces. The reason being: no goal or focus at the helm. The same need for attention applies to each of us.

It is also important that you develop strong habits to ensure that you are constantly working toward your goal. Just merely setting a goal is not enough. Equally vital is goal-getting by action-taking.

3. *Remove Distractions*

What types of distractions? Any and all distractions and this includes the drama kings and queens in your life. Let me digress for a second. You know who I am talking about: the whiners, the victims, the woe-is-me types. We all know a few, and if you do not know any, then you are *that* person.

In my case, I took a look at my list, then slashed and burned. The drama kings and queens were falling like bowling pins. *And what if this person is my spouse?* I hear some of you sheepishly asking. Sorry, but you may just have to bid farewell to him or her as well. Tough to accept, but true. Listen, changing your life is serious business. Sissies need not apply! You need all the positive energy you can assemble around you.

Now, back to the point I am making. Time to properly prioritize your activities. Proponents of successful behaviour all agree: activities that provide the highest return are the ones to be performed. Be honest with yourself. Is listening to and entertaining your whiny siblings causing you to jump with enthusiasm? Is watching that new television program getting you closer to your goals?

Another thing is that we like to be *in the know*, so we allow ourselves to be barraged with information from the media. Let me tell you something. Most of that information is negative and outside of your influence. It is also time-consuming and irrelevant to your goals.

If you want things in your life to change, you have to change things in your life. It is more than just merely wanting to change your life. You *decide* to change your life. This is you doing whatever it takes, whenever it takes and for however long it takes.

I am obsessed with my goal. I do not allow any interruptions when I am performing goal-related activities. This means that I am associating with other high-caliber, positive and successful goal-oriented people. I am following a plan of action that is referenced and followed at all times, including staying away from gossip and anything of that nature. It amazes me how much precious time is spent on minding other peoples' business, entertaining family dramas, or seeking approval from people who are yet to find their way to their dreams.

4. *Monitor Your Progress*

Take stock by checking to see if your actions are getting you closer to your desires and goals. This is one of the most accurate measures of where you are on your journey. Do this regularly: daily, weekly and monthly. Or, if you are like me, do it each minute. *A bit much*, you might say.

Remember, we must be vigilant in order to be successful. We have a tendency to go way over the top when it comes to participating in the follies of the world. However, when it comes to doing something constructive like checking to see if we are in line with our goals, we tend to view it as being *too much*.

Socrates stated that "an unexamined life is not worth living." Examine yourself to see if you are headed in the direction that helps you to fulfill your potential. Seek out the help of an honest friend or associate and ask him or her to provide you with feedback. And above all, maintain faith in yourself. No matter the circumstances, always have faith in yourself. Even when appearances seem contradictory, believe that you will reap the reward of your efforts.

Always focus on what you desire.

*~ **Andy Shaw***

Chapter 3

Teachability: The True Indicator

Enter into the discipline necessary to bring about a radical change in your life. Do so deliberately. Then allow nothing to interfere with your decision.

~ Charles F. Haanel

ATTENTION, PLEASE!! IT'S separation time. Let's separate the doers from the talkers. The warriors from the wimps. The champs from the chumps. The committed from the drifters.

Believe me! You will know, without a shadow of a doubt, the category to which you belong once the concept of teachability is dissected and explained. For simplicity, I will reference John C. Maxwell. In his book *Thinking for a Change*, he described teachability as "an attitude." So, before we go any further, it is imperative that you understand teachability as being an attitude that YOU possess.

The Teachability Index

Now the extent to which you are teachable (coachable) depends on how you rank on what is known as the teachability index. This index has two variables. In order to be considered teachable, you have to rank high in both. Not just one. Both!! Your willingness to learn and your willingness to change.

Normally, I would do this at the end of the chapter. However, given the importance of this topic, I am hereby stating the following premise: There is a direct correlation between your level of teachability and your level of success. The more teachable you are, the more successful you will become. It is vital that you keep this in mind as you read along. Your teachability level is the True Indicator of your success or lack thereof. Are you ready to see how you stack up?

First variable on the teachability index: an individual's willingness to learn. *Derian, how do I know the extent of my willingness to learn the things that will help get me closer to achieving my dreams?*

My answer is: First and foremost, by what you are willing to give in return for your goals and dreams. In other words, are you willing to forego your favourite television program for three months in order to attend night classes so that you can become a nurse, if that is your dream? Are you willing to invest some money to pay for information that will provide key insights on how to go about achieving whatever it is you want to achieve? Better yet, are you willing to reschedule your annual Mexican vacation so that you can attend a sales seminar that will be in your neck of the woods during the same time as your planned trip to Mexico? Seriously, what is worth changing up for your dream?

Nothing Sacred

For me, it is anything and everything. Nothing is off limits. I am a firm believer that your *willingness* is the indicator for how much you want something. I remember when I made the decision to pursue an accounting certification with the intention that it would help me to advance in my professional career.

The program I chose entailed me being in class all day on Saturdays for the first eight months. The remaining six days during that time were spent doing tons of homework assignments, and there never seemed to be enough time to get them all done. At the same time, I was working a full-time job at a law firm, which had its own demands – let us just say I worked lots of overtime.

Clearly a few things had to give. But I really wanted to get ahead in my professional career and becoming a certified accountant would contribute to my ascension up the corporate ladder. So, what did I give up in order to accomplish this goal? Let's see. Weekly date nights with my wife. All forms of television. Sleep. The gym (and I LOVE the gym).

To provide a clearer picture, here was my schedule for those wonderful first eight months. I attended classes from 8am to 4pm on Saturdays. Took an hour break to gather myself when I got home. Began doing homework assignments from 6pm that same evening and all day on Sunday. Went to work from 8am to 5pm on Monday to Friday. And from 5:30pm until 10:30pm on those nights, I stayed at work and did the remainder of my homework assignments. At 10:40pm, I took the last bus and got home at around 11:45pm. Went to bed around 1am and repeated the process the next day. It was intense, but I greatly wanted to advance my career and this was the price I was willing to pay. Life became a bit more manageable after the first eight months, but I still had to forego many things over the remaining 18 months.

Looking back, I guess I gave up more than weekly date nights. It seemed like I had given up the entire relationship with my wife. My dream was more important to me than anything else. And because I had a strong and intense desire to climb the corporate ladder, I was willing to make huge sacrifices along the way. My willingness to learn was extremely high because I was willing to give up anything in return for my dream. It's okay. You can go ahead and judge me on my priorities.

Many people claim they want to be successful, but they do not want to give anything in return. They cannot fathom trading unproductive activities for the pursuit of a dream they have been fantasizing about for what seems like an eternity.

If you are not willing to give up anything in return for your dream, you are not as willing to learn as you may think you are. And consequently, if you do not rank highly on the willingness-to-learn scale, your teachability index is low. Which means you are not that teachable. Which means you will experience little to no success in your life.

Remember the direct correlation between your level of teachability and your level of success that I mentioned earlier? Those who are the most teachable are willing to give anything and do whatever it takes in order to achieve their goals.

If your goal is to lose weight – I use this as an example because it seems that most people have this as a dream – you would be willing to give up your favourite dessert at the local pastry shop. Or, you would be willing to give up an extra hour of sleep to attend the gym at 5am.

Willingness

People who are willing to learn are willing to *pay the price* to achieve whatever they set out to do. In the case of my goal to become a certified accountant, the price was a decrease in leisure and relaxation time, as well as giving up fun activities with my wife. What price are you willing to pay? What are you willing to give up?

Second variable on the teachability index: Dear Reader, if you felt the first variable was challenging – that is, willingness to learn – this one is downright difficult. It is your willingness to accept change. Ooooh!! *Change?* Just the mere mention of the word causes people to break out in hives. I can hear the stampede of feet running toward the door because people resist change like Superman avoids kryptonite.

You might be willing to learn, but to change? NO! NO!! NO!!! This is of no interest to you. Thus, you choose comfort and so-called security at the expense of your dreams. This is not a holier-than-thou attitude on my part. I am just stating the facts as I see them.

What does willingness to accept change really mean? It means being willing to change your self-defeating beliefs into new life-altering beliefs. It means discarding old habits and developing new habits to help you in the pursuit of your dreams.

To put it more bluntly, it means that you are willing to do things way differently than you have been doing up to this point in your life. It requires your willingness to deal with discomfort, because pursuing your dream will be a very uncomfortable undertaking. Otherwise, everyone would be living their dreams right this very moment.

Let me digress and ease your fears a bit by telling you that dealing with change can be made simple if you have a compelling reason to go through the uncomfortable process. Ben Arment, author of *Dream Year,* refers to this compelling reason as the "inciting incident." It is that one thing or issue that confronts a person and sets his or her story in motion.

Enough is Enough

Fortunately (or unfortunately, depending on how you look at it), I had two inciting incidents that spurred me on in my pursuit of attaining financial freedom. The first was my brother's death in 2001. At thirteen years old, my brother developed a heart condition and died six months later. During those six months, I watched as my parents stressed about financial decisions.

Now, I am not claiming that my brother would have remained alive even if money was readily available. However, key decisions could have been made sooner, thus giving him a better chance of survival. I vowed to never undergo that experience again.

This inciting incident was a catalyst for me to begin thinking differently; for deciding to create surplus funds in my experience, as opposed to barely having enough to get by in life. What if I was faced with a similar situation regarding my child as my parents had with my brother?

The pain of losing my younger brother, coupled with an intense desire to be able to care for my daughter in the event that some illness came upon her, provided a strong motivation for me to change the way I had always thought about life up to that point. I had to think differently and, more importantly, do things differently, in order to put me in a financially independent position. Although changing my mind-set was uncomfortable, it was nothing compared to what I endured in losing my brother. So, I was willing to do whatever it took to experience more money in my life.

The second inciting incident occurred after I began climbing the corporate ladder, when I noticed a complete lack of fulfillment and freedom in my life. Again, I had a strong desire. I wanted out of the Rat Race. So, I had to shift my mindset yet again: from employee to business owner. I was willing to give up the comfort of a pay cheque in return for the reward of doing something that I loved to do... something that gives me tons of satisfaction and allows me to live life on my own terms. I was willing to change the way I thought about life as well as step up my capability of becoming the very best version of myself. And for you, what is your inciting incident?

How Do You Score?

Ask yourself the following: *Am I willing to get uncomfortable enough in the pursuit of my dreams? How badly do I want it?* I came across the following quote by Jen Sincero, personal coach and author. I am sharing it with you because I find it to be a perfect observation of people regarding their willingness to accept change. Jen states: "Lots of people wish for change, really, really want it, are willing to invest the time and money into it but are ultimately not willing to get uncomfortable enough to actually make anything happen. Which means they don't want it as badly as they say they do."

Jen continues: "People who are successful are not only willing to get uncomfortable, but they know they have to make a habit of it if they want to stay successful... it's the willingness to keep pushing through new challenges that separates the successful from the unsuccessful."

To add to Jen's latter statement, I am sure you have heard the phrase: "short-term pain for long-term gain." In actuality, the pain only becomes an issue if you do not resolve to face up to, and deal with, any and all challenges and obstacles. I can share with you the countless stories about being uncomfortable and pushing through many obstacles in my pursuit of getting involved in the field of real estate. And these were just from the exercises that my mentor put me through.

There were other obstacles such as getting financing from the bank, dealing with insurance companies, and the day-to-day operations coupled with tenant issues. I also had limited cash flow at the beginning. But those stories are not my focus at this time. My focus is to help you examine yourself to determine how you score on the teachability index.

So, how teachable are you? How committed are you in the pursuit of your dreams? What are you willing to do in return for success? Are you willing to make sacrifices? How about your social life? What about your golf game? Are you willing to change old self-defeating habits for new productive habits?

If you want a new life with new circumstances, you have to do the work, rather than simply wishing and wanting. While the *wishful* enjoy the idea of success, the *willful* enjoy the actions that lead to real success. This is where the rubber meets the road. This is where the true warriors rise and the phonies are discarded.

Being low on the teachability scale is the number one reason for failure; fear is not the main reason as you were taught to believe. Some people just flatly refuse to give up anything in return for their dreams. Or they are unwilling to change old thought patterns. To echo the sentiments of Jen Sincero, they just do not want success badly enough. They are not very teachable, hence the reason why success seems to elude them time and time again.

What This Means to You

You may have a hard time accepting this, but dreaming is the easy part of the equation. It is the work to achieve your dream that is difficult. However, the work half of the equation can be made less daunting if you work on becoming more teachable. Being teachable has many facets.

In the short term, you may need to give up some of your favourite activities in order to achieve your dream. Think about how to do things differently than how you are accustomed. You may change some of your friends. You will find that the excuses and distractions that have prevented you from taking bold action will disappear. You will find yourself making a complete overhaul of your life.

For me, this process involved renovating my life. I was unable to attend some family activities. *Isn't spending time with family a good thing?* Yes, but not when all of us are broke. My aim was to change my life and become successful, not to be a willing participant in the Broke Convention with my family and friends. Sorry!

I stopped surfing the internet. I also stopped watching television. The way I saw it, I was spending time watching other people pursuing their dreams while all I had to show for myself were red eyes and a hollow head from watching too much TV. I get it! It is tough to let go of old thought patterns and habits. Just because it is tough does not mean you can't do it. This is where being teachable is important. I heard it said somewhere that your attitude determines your altitude. And remember, teachability is an attitude. It is an attitude that is directly correlated with success.

I am sharing my knowledge and experiences with you to relay the message that anyone can become more teachable. I am changing my habits. You can change your habits too. Take it from me. I am not smarter than you. I am not more talented than you. I am not prettier than you. Hold on, maybe I am prettier. I am kidding! Just wanted to make sure you are still paying attention. When you are willing to learn and willing to accept change, I can guarantee you that your life will never be the same. It will be better and better.

Here are tips to improve both variables:

1. **Determine and acknowledge where you are on the teachability scale right now.**

Yes, an honest assessment is always the beginning.

2. **Once you acknowledge your area of weakness, focus on the next immediate step for you.**

The next immediate step will mean different things to different people. We are not all at the same stage. For example, the next step for one person could be hiring a mentor or a coach to help them decide what it is they want to achieve. Another person may already know what he or she wants to accomplish, so their next step is simply to begin, and could also include hiring a mentor or coach to help by keeping them accountable.

3. *Surround yourself with people who have already achieved what you are aiming to achieve.*

By seeing other people in action, your desire and belief in your own ability to achieve will be raised. And once your belief and desire are raised, your willingness to learn and accept change will increase. Which means your teachability index will go up. Which means you become more teachable as a result. Tah dah!!

4. *Do something different each day.*

Take a different route to your place of employment each day for the next week. Or do something that scares the crap out of you. This exercise helps you to increase your willingness to accept change; your willingness to do things differently. It also helps with you being more comfortable with discomfort. It is all about practice, practice, practice, and every little thing helps.

*The greatest obstacle to growth is not ignorance
but the illusion of knowledge.*

~ John C. Maxwell

Chapter 4

Mentorship: The Blueprint

*He that is taught only by himself
has a fool for his master.*

~ Ben Jonson, Playwright

FIND A MENTOR! Would you take advice from a farmer if your goal was to be a doctor? Maybe the farmer knows a thing or two about medicine, but could you really consider him to be an expert in health care? On that note, if your goal is to achieve a certain type of success, why would you listen to someone who has never achieved the kind of success you are after? If you do, you are setting yourself up for failure before you even get started.

I won't beat around the bush. You must listen to and learn from those who already have what you want or have already achieved whatever is it that you are after in the field of your choice. Plain and simple. Choosing one of these people to be your mentor is vitally important. This entire chapter talks about the value and benefit of having a mentor.

A Blueprint to Success

A mentor provides a path for the destination you are aiming to reach. A combination of detailed knowledge and personal introductions to a vast array of contacts will become readily available to you. Having a mentor saves you time. Without a mentor, making these connections would probably take you many years to establish. Following in the footsteps of others is a simple life success hack. You will still have to put in the work, because, as you know, your dreams will never manifest by you sitting on your rear. Having a mentor helps you to channel your energy in the right kind of action. Having a mentor has enabled me to get privileged access to great projects when I ventured into real estate investing, since the best deals are not announced to the public.

When it came to getting connected, all it took was an introduction from my mentor. Lawyers, brokers, accountants, bankers and other types of professionals were available to me, ready to provide services that would help me advance closer to my goals. Can you fathom the time, effort and money it would have taken me to establish these relationships on my own?

Now, when doing something for the first time, we feel the need to go at it alone, reinvent the wheel and figure out things by ourselves. We are running around thinking that we have to add our own touch and flare to something before truly knowing what it is about or what we are doing. Stop! Don't give in to the temptation. An upside to having a mentor is that he or she comes with resources and systems that can be readily employed. Your responsibility at this point is to utilize and master them, while honouring the confidence of your mentor in you.

A Next-Level You

Some call it being a better version of yourself. Whatever you call it, a mentor helps you on that journey of personal transformation. You often hear that life is more than the things you achieve, it is about the person who you become through the process.

While I was an employee in the corporate world, I had a mentor who ensured my participation in meetings and other events that provided me with insight into the systems and culture of the organization.

My mentor taught me both what to think, and how to think. Do you understand the difference? Life lessons that he emphasized for success in achieving goals and dreams are trust, honesty, integrity, and teamwork. Further, I learned the type of questions to ask, how to ask them and how to actively listen. Your ability with this latter component pre-determines the level of your success.

What Not to Do

A mentor saves you heartache. In addition to providing you with recommendations on your path to success, a mentor also teaches you what not to do. He or she would have already made mistakes and so is in a great position to inform / advise you of the pitfalls to avoid. Ignorance is costly. You will definitely benefit from hearing about the lessons that your mentor has learned along the way... the successes and the failures.

As an example, during the early years, in order to gain access to capital, I would entertain doing business with anyone who showed the slightest interest in wanting to partner up with me on a project. My mentor informed me of the inherent risk in this behaviour. He pointed out that what I was doing could lead to a potentially successful project becoming a perpetual nightmare. He then explained the importance of qualifying investors. It was not the quantity, but quality of people.

The basic premise is: do not chase money. I was told that business partnerships or joint ventures are akin to a marriage. If the foundation is based solely on money, then the entire thing will fall apart. He taught me that money was a good servant, but not a good master. His advice was spot on because I later learned from mutual associates that some of the people with whom I had considered joining forces were terrible business partners. It was great to side-step those potential detours on my path.

Accountability

Accountability leads to improved performance. I knew I had to answer to someone and knowing that I had to attain a high level of proficiency really kept me focused. Periodic feedback and suggestions enabled me to improve my skills and my level of personal growth. Oh, before I forget, let me state something of utmost importance: even though you may not always agree with your mentor, I strongly suggest that you follow his / her advice to the letter.

Do not attempt to do things your own way. Let me say this again! Do not attempt to do things your own way. There will be a time for your own way, just not at the beginning stage. You will first have to earn your proverbial stripes.

When I started out, I followed my mentor's instructions intently, and asked questions for clarification as needed. It was only after three years of meticulously following his advice and continuously taking action on the things he suggested, that I began to offer my opinions. However, by that time, I had earned this right. I had built up a solid reputation of being coachable and teachable so my mentor was willing to entertain my ideas. As it pertains to you, learn to master the basics of what your mentor has taught you before going off and putting your own spin on things.

Reduce Isolation

It is important to note that the road to failure is cluttered with many who will carefully explain why something can't be done. You may find it increasingly difficult to communicate with and be around this type of person. You will find that your mentor is an invaluable resource for positive feedback and in building momentum.

A sense of partnership is created when working with someone who shares the same ideas as you, which then leads to reducing your feeling of isolation at times. Your mentor would most likely have gone through similar feelings. As a result, your mentor can assist you in how to handle such situations.

As an example, my mentor explained to me that my journey is mine alone and not like the journey of anyone else. As a result, I do not need the approval of others. He reminded me that most people follow popular thinking to nowhere. The fact that I was choosing to do things differently meant that I was willing to stand out; that I was choosing the path less travelled, which is ultimately the path that leads to freedom. This affirmation led to a renewed focus on my part, with me advancing confidently in the direction I had chosen. At the same time, I noticed that naysayers were having less and less of an effect on my life because through my mentor, I was being introduced to new people sharing similarly supportive views as my own.

Broad Perspective

Due to a mentor's wider experience and vision, you, as a mentee, will be able to stretch your thinking. This is where I saw the most improvement in my personal development. As a matter of fact, it seemed as though I acquired much of the thinking, mannerisms and characteristics of my mentor. In listening to the stories from his experiences, my imagination soared and I began to think of all the new and positive possibilities that could come about in my life. No longer did I focus on the obstacles that might prevent me from achieving my dreams. I was exposed to new paradigms and this created rewarding results both personally and in business.

Canvas to Test Ideas

Everyone needs a sounding board and having a mentor enables you to test your ideas and discuss your points of view with an engaged listener. The fact that your mentor is not in competition with you means that you can be confident that your ideas will not be stolen. And because he / she is supportive of you, judgement is suspended. You can speak and operate freely and safely.

It is refreshing to take an idea to your mentor and, together, you tweak, revise, expand and eventually you are ready to take action on the idea. While some ideas may be discarded altogether, at least they were taken at face value.

No idea is deemed useless. Your mentor points out things that you may not have taken into account, such as potential barriers or legal considerations. My point is that a mentor both supports your interests and is willing to assist you in bringing them to fruition.

Pay It Forward

Lastly, and maybe the most rewarding thing for your mentor to witness, is when you, in turn, become a mentor to someone else. The student has now become the master. The experience of working with my mentor served as a training ground. The knowledge that I have gained from my mentor is imparted on others within my circle. The more I share this knowledge, the more joy I feel. As for my mentor, he gets a sense of accomplishment in watching me apply and share the concepts that I have learned, and continue to learn, from him.

To recap, I began by stating that you do best to only listen to individuals who have already achieved the things you would like to achieve. Heed the words of playwright Ben Jonson, who said, "He that is taught only by himself has a fool for a master."

Here is the part where I help you out:

How do you go about finding the right mentor?

Ask! It is that simple. If the individual whom you admire and want to emulate is someone you have access to – that is, he or she is within close proximity to you – then ask him or her to mentor you. They will gladly take you on, especially if they get the sense that you are serious about whatever it is you want to achieve.

Successful people obtain real pleasure in passing on their knowledge and expertise to others. It is their way of giving back. They relish the opportunity to be a mentor. So, take your chances. Have the courage to ask and offer some form of exchange.

What if the person does not want to mentor me?

It rarely ever happens that someone will decline to be your mentor. As I said, people who have achieved anything of merit receive great personal satisfaction in passing on to others what they have learned. This is legacy in action. They are generally flattered to be seen as an inspiration and are happy to answer questions on themselves and their achievements.

What if I don't know anyone who has achieved the things I want to achieve?

You do not have to personally know your mentor. *But doesn't this contradict the point of this message*? No! *How so?* Because you can get a mentor from books. Yes, good ol' books.

Read the biography and autobiography of someone who you want to emulate. For example, if you want to be great piano player, read the biographies and autobiographies of great pianists. The same applies if you want to be a successful chef, or policeman, or florist. Whatever it is you want to be, do or have, I can bet you that someone else has found their way to the goal in your sights.

By the way, your mentor can be someone who is deceased. How many American Presidents yearn to be like Abraham Lincoln, even though he died in 1865? And how many scientists still look up to Albert Einstein? In the field of sports, some young kid believes that he is the next Babe Ruth. In body-building, you may want to develop abs like those of Ryan Gosling! Get the point?

How can I convince someone to mentor me?

Take initiative. Be willing to take action, no matter how small. And do so using the resources around you, no matter how little. To borrow the words of my grandfather, "People cannot help but help someone who is taking action – going in the direction of their dreams."

Life success hack: Choose a mentor!

> *What we do for ourselves alone dies with us, but what we do for others remains and is immortal.*
>
> **~ John C. Maxwell**

SECTION 2

The Accelerators

Chapter 5

Appreciation: The Catalyst

*Appreciation is the highest form of prayer, for it acknowledges
the presence of good wherever you shine the light of
your thankful thoughts.*

~ Alan Cohen

BEFORE I DELVE into the topic of Appreciation, there are a couple of things I would like to bring to your attention.

Firstly, the words *Appreciation*, *Gratitude* and *Thankful* will be used interchangeably for ease of purpose. Secondly, let me take the time to apologize in advance of losing my cool in certain sections of this chapter. I have very little tolerance for unappreciative people. So, when I refer to whiners and those who love to complain, I might be a little harsh. That virus they carry around is one that I certainly do not want to catch. So, please bear with me and understand that I, too, still have areas in my life which need improvement. Anyway, let us get started on the concept of being Appreciative and what it means to you being successful in achieving your dreams and desires.

Appreciation is simply acceptance: acceptance of what is. In other words, you accept things as they are. As a result, the feeling of struggle is dissipated. This means you are no longer worried or anxious, which means your energy is now flowing freely. Your focus is in the *present* and you are shaping your life in the manner you imagine.

Help Yourself by Being Thankful

The more appreciative you are, the better your life will be. And what does being appreciative entail? It means being Thankful for everything that you already have. When you are Thankful, you are essentially summoning the Universe – or God – to send you more things for Appreciation.

In this state of Thankfulness and Appreciation, you open yourself up and bring into your life more wonderful things and amazing experiences! Being appreciative is simply you being aware of the many good things in your life.

Each morning as I arise, I immediately give thanks for my countless blessings. I continue this process throughout the entire day and it has evolved to the point where I now document these items in a notebook. And from time to time, I will go through this book and just reread some of the things that I have expressed thanks for in the past. This exercise keeps me focused on the positive situations and circumstances that I have encountered throughout my life as well as those that I am encountering now.

Being Grateful enables me to reflect on all the wins and successes that I have achieved, hence, there is no time for me to become fearful, worried, doubtful or anxious.

Here is a little secret. You cannot focus on two things at the exact same time – and please don't let misguided multi-taskers tell you otherwise. By being in a constant state of Appreciation, you diminish the chance of negative emotions popping up.

What are some of the things for which I am Thankful and Appreciative? My life. My family. My granddaughter (she tops the list). Food on my table. Clothes on my back. My ability to think. Great friendships. Good Music. Fresh Air. A bed in which to sleep. By the way, has there ever been any better invention than a comfy bed? A good massage ranks second after being with my granddaughter. The fact that I have eyes to see. Legs to walk. And the list goes on and on. Even more importantly, I am also Appreciative and Thankful for the so-called bad or undesirable events that occur in my life. The storms of life, so to speak. *Derian, are you insane? How can you be thankful when undesirable things happen to you?*

First of all, I do not view anything as a bad event. I see them as opportunities. In fact, I am of the view that undesirable events are actually good things in disguise. Secondly, my Appreciation for this type of incident allows me to grow by opening me up to the lessons they bring. Let me give you an example.

A Life-Changing Event

Just after I turned eighteen years old, I was selected for a scholarship to attend a university abroad. I was excited. The world appeared to be at my feet. A few months later, my girlfriend told me that she was pregnant.

Now, I am going to be brutally honest. When you are eighteen years old and you find out you are about to have a baby, you are not jumping for joy. As a matter of fact, the first thing I thought was, "Damn, my parents are going to kill me." Well, if I am being honest as I proclaimed, I thought more along the lines that my parents were going to #&$! me up. In addition, I also thought about what would happen to my scholarship. In any event, I composed myself right away and decided that I would forego my scholarship – and, if I was still alive after telling my parents of the pregnancy – I was going to be a great father to my yet-to-be-born child.

So, first there was an acceptance of the situation. Once I accepted the current circumstances, I was no longer worried about the repercussions. Fearful? Yes. But worried? No! There is a difference. I was fearful because I did not know what to expect. After all, I had never had a child before (and so far, this is the only one). But I was not worried because I told myself that whatever was ahead of me, I would face it head on.

I immediately thought that the timing of my girlfriend's pregnancy could be for some specific reason and maybe it needed to happen this way so I could learn some sort of lesson. For one, maybe I needed to learn that no one is immune to teenage pregnancy or other unfortunate (or, yes, fortunate) events.

And learn I did. I learned not to pass judgement on anyone. I learned to have empathy. I learned the hardships of being a young father. Damn! That was the toughest lesson. But most importantly, I learned how to be an excellent father. Which brings me to this point: How can I not be appreciative of that? How can I not be appreciative of this situation when it helped me become a better person?

Having a baby at a young age forced me to embrace maturity. It forced me to grow up. Listen, I am not advocating or campaigning for teenage pregnancy. I am just sharing my experience to make a point that you can also be appreciative for seemingly catastrophic events in your life.

Greatest Tragedy

Most people – please tell me that you are not one of them – are always focusing on the things that are lacking in their lives instead of being Thankful for the things they have. If you are guilty of this habit, please resolve to immediately discard it. As Schopenhauer so bluntly exclaimed, "We seldom think of what we have but always of what we lack." This tendency is the greatest tragedy on earth. Do not permit or allow your mind to be in a permanent state of dissatisfaction with the way things presently are. You will only attract and bring more of that – dissatisfaction.

We tend to be chronic complainers. I know people who constantly whine about the weather. One time it is too cold. Another time, it is too rainy. Or too hot. Or too windy. Too much snow, and on and on. Simply Appreciate the fact that you are alive to experience the many different faces of Mother Nature. Be Grateful that you are able to feel the elements in all their glory. And if the weather is still such an issue for you, go live in a bubble. Chances are you will complain about the bubble too. Look, I told you I have little tolerance for complainers.

We also like to talk about our health issues. It is as though we are competing for the Sad Story of the Year Award. Instead of complaining about aches and pains, we can give thanks that we have eyes to see. Give thanks that we can walk. For goodness' sake, give thanks that we can speak so that we are able to complain. In any circumstance, we all have something for which we can be Thankful.

So, next time the urge arises to whine and complain about something not going your way, express Appreciation instead. Think of one thing for which you are Thankful. Plato said: "A grateful mind is a great mind which eventually attracts to itself great things."

Conversely, you make things worse for yourself when you fail to acknowledge the wonderful gifts you are currently receiving. What incentive does the Universe have to send you more gifts, if you are not in Appreciation of the gifts it is sending you now?

At times, instead of being Grateful, you are in the manufacturing business. You manufacture your own unhappiness. Things do not have to be perfect for you to enjoy and Appreciate them. For example, I used to hate standing in line, whether it is at the supermarket, at the bank, or anywhere, for that matter. My distaste for this activity was so great that I would become restless and grumpy or I would get annoyed.

Eventually, it dawned on me that I was manufacturing my own unhappiness. I was only harming my spirit. So, I quickly decided to use the so-called wasted time to reflect on my life instead. Right away I thought about how fast-paced my life seemed to be. It then occurred to me that standing in line provided me an opportunity to slow down and to get in touch with who I really am. I began reflecting on my goals and how close I am to achieving them. In observing my surroundings, I had a glimpse of how other people were losing their wits. I vowed to never become like them, and to develop some patience and compassion (God knows I need that).

My new perspective about waiting in line extended to other things such as sitting in traffic. I grew to Appreciate and be Thankful for these moments as well that are great times to decompress, listen to some good music, or go *inside* myself. Caution! The sitting-in-traffic thing only works if you are alone in the car. Having someone else present with you could highlight the difference between you channeling your inner Buddha or you realizing you are capable of being completely intolerant. You can't say I did not warn you. You'll be amazed how the people closest to you can drive you up the wall when you are both in a car, stuck in traffic.

Anyway, the point is that we can learn to be Grateful for everything in life: the pleasant and the not-so-pleasant. When the Gratitude habit is cultivated, everything we need to bring about our dreams and desires is continuously flowing toward us.

Again, an appreciative mind attracts great things. By the way, do you have a tendency to take others for granted? Do you often say "Thank you" to the people whom you really Appreciate, and regularly to people in general?

Hey, I will admit that I was guilty of taking others for granted. While I would think about how much these people meant to me, I never bothered to tell them. And that was a pity. Today, it is quite the opposite. Every chance I get, I express my Appreciation to those who have touched my life in some way. As if by magic, I notice more and more how quality individuals are entering my life each day, and the ones who were there from the beginning want to remain a part of my life. How beautiful is that? I know you might think that this is airy-fairy stuff, but it works. It's so simple, yet so powerful! Give it a try and observe how great you feel.

Appreciation and Your Dreams

So, how exactly does showing Appreciation help with the achievement of your dreams and desires? Well, quite frankly, it strengthens your faith. And as you learned in Chapter 1, faith is a big component in achieving your dreams and desires. When you show Appreciation – or when you express Gratitude – you are essentially demonstrating your utmost confidence that all is well and that all will continue to be well.

As your confidence increases, fear and doubt disappear. As fear and doubt leave the vicinity, your belief that you can achieve the object of your desire steps in (more on this in an upcoming chapter). Once belief makes its presence felt, you will act with focused intention, knowing that everything you imagine is possible. Tah dah!

Now, follow me closely as I reveal a little tidbit. I stated earlier that each time you show Appreciation, you are telling the Universe to send you more things that provide you with that same feeling. The Universe will deliver. Now, if you are constantly having feelings of Appreciation for everything in your life, and therefore the Universe *has* to respond in kind, what does that mean? It means you will achieve your dreams, because achieving your dreams is one such thing that will make you feel appreciative. Get it? In essence, you are already living your dream. The future is now. You have achieved it, whatever IT is. And this, my friend, is how showing Appreciation – being Thankful – helps you in the achievement of your dreams and desires. And when they are achieved, then you get to set new goals!

Action Exercises

1. Each day, be Thankful for what you have and for who you are, no matter your current situation, because the Universe evidently provides abundantly when we are in a state of Appreciation. So, make a conscious effort to focus on what you have rather than on what you think you are lacking.

2. Throughout your day, say the following, often: "I am Thankful for all that I had in the past. I am Thankful for all that I have now. And I am Thankful for all that I shall have in the future."

3. When something goes wrong or something bad happens, stop and ask yourself, "What can I learn from this? Where is the opportunity in this event that will enable me to become a stronger individual?"

Again, you might dismiss this as airy-fairy madness. *I think Derian has lost his marbles.* But cynicism and skepticism will not do you any good. You can continue to do things your way, with mediocre results, or you can apply the concept discussed in this chapter and live an abundant, fulfilling life. Which will you choose?

The first step toward discarding a scarcity mentality involves giving thanks for everything that you have.

~ Dr. Wayne Dyer

Chapter 6

Giving: The Generator of Riches

We cannot obtain what we lack if we tenaciously cling to what we have.

~ Charles F. Haanel

I was somewhat reluctant to write on the concept of *Giving* because of the intricacies involved. I felt like I would not be able to do the subject justice. Also, for most of my life, I struggled with the lessons of this Universal Law, and what I now see as a life success hack. However, a little over a decade ago, I decided to make a concerted effort to put the law into practice. Since then, many opportunities have come my way and good things just always seem to happen to me. As a result, of all the chapters, this particular chapter gave me the most pleasure to compose, as the insight I gained pertaining to this concept has been the single biggest contributor to my success.

Definitions

I refer to *Giving* as the *Generator of Riches*. Stated another way, it is the dynamo that enables the things you desire to come to you. When done under the right conditions, the habit of giving automatically aligns you with the Universe. Everything that you could ever imagine will flow to you in ways you will never fathom. Before I go any further, let me define a few terms as they pertain to the subject.

Riches are hereby defined as being both tangible and intangible. *Riches* are not solely represented by money, cars and other luxurious items. The term also includes love, happiness, joy, and peace of mind; in other words, things that can only be felt within.

The same applies to *Giving*, which can be carried out in numerous forms. Although usually assessed from a monetary standpoint, you can also give love, your time, compliments, encouraging words to someone, and through doing more work than for which you are paid.

Debunking the Myth

Now, I feel compelled to dispel the fallacy of a certain accepted fact. I am sure you have heard, "It is far better to give than to receive." It is not true! Let me emphasize: That statement is inaccurate! Both *giving* and *receiving* are equally necessary in order for the law to work, thus resulting in positive outcomes for you. Neither one takes precedence over the other, as one person's giving is another person's receiving. We live in a Universe of duality and just like breathing in and then exhaling out, giving and receiving depend upon each other.

Thus, if you are in the habit of refusing things from others, you are slamming shut the door of abundance and prosperity (of all kinds) that are yearning to come to you. Increasing our willingness to *receive* expands our capacity to *give*.

I had a chip on my shoulder that I did not ever want to be indebted to anyone. I did not want to feel like I owed anybody anything.

One day, a very lovely lady challenged my ignorant outlook regarding receiving assistance from others. She asked me to describe the feeling that overtakes me when I give my resources or my time to others. With my holier-than-thou disposition, I smiled from ear-to-ear and responded, "Great! It makes me feel all warm inside."

She then remarked, "So why are you so determined to prevent someone else from experiencing that same wonderful feeling?" While I was searching for a rebuttal, the lady went on to remark that my refusal to accept good things from others meant that I was looking the gift horse in the mouth, which would decrease the amount of great and wonderful things appearing to enrich my life.

The Universe, or God, or whatever name you ascribe, is the gift horse. That lady's words left a lasting impression on me. So much so that, today, when anyone asks me my profession, I tell them that I am an Excellent Receiver. Seriously! You should see the look on their faces after hearing that. Over the past several years I have become more proficient at *receiving*, with each year bringing even bigger miracles. The following is an example.

I welcomed my granddaughter, Nadia, into the world on April 27, 2014. The overwhelming support that my family received was "gi-normous." Almost a year later, the gifts were still coming, in the form of Pampers and clothing, and more. I doubt this would have been the case had I continued to hold onto my previous belief regarding *receiving*.

The Nuances

Congratulations! We have debunked the myth that it is far better to give than to receive, so let us now focus our attention on the concept of *Giving* itself.

By sharing what you have, you permit the abundant Universe to send gifts your way. When you give of yourself or your resources, you are essentially saying that you believe in the abundance of the Universe, as opposed to believing there is lack of any kind. This is a powerful statement that will work wonders for you.

Now, how you *feel* when you give is key. Give with joy. In order to give with joy, it has to be about something that moves your heart. That way, you are apt to give more freely. Your feelings and emotions are what activate the law to work for or against you. When giving, do so with no reservations whatsoever. If you are not feeling good about giving, or you are giving only for what you believe you will get in return, you have an equation / transaction mentality. And this, my friend, violates the law.

Keep in mind that your returns will not necessarily come from the people who you originally assisted. Your returns will come from sources that you would not have expected in your wildest dreams. Also, the returns may not be in the same form as your original offering.

For example, each month, I make monetary donations to one of my favourite children's charities. In return, I receive inspiration from the stories of survival by some of the kids. I also receive confidence that these children will one day grow up and do their part to make our world a better place in which to live. And finally, I develop a deeper sense of Appreciation for the many blessings in my life. In my opinion, these things have more value than my monetary donations.

Pay close attention because you do not want to miss what I am about to tell you. Give what you want to receive. So, if you want to receive love, show love. If you want money, give money. If you want more energy, exert energy. If you want more peace, live peacefully. *But doesn't this contradict what you stated in the previous paragraph about my returns not necessarily being in the same form as my original offering?* No! Here's why.

Firstly, I said the returns *may not* be in the same form. I did not say they *will not* be in the same form as your original currency. Secondly, when I originally made the donation to the children's charity, I had no care in the world about what came back in return. Whatever the Universe saw fit to give me, I was willing to accept. This attitude meant that I always ended up getting better stuff because I received things that were in my best good. Let this swirl around in your head some more. This is why I requested that you pay closer attention, by the way.

But Wait! The Rules

Oh yes! There are a couple of rules pertaining to the subject of *Giving* that are imperative for you to always follow. My aim is to help you understand how your act – there is that word again – of *Giving* translates into taking action on your dreams and desires. *Giving* must be done under the proper conditions for the law to work to your benefit. I do not want you to go around giving all willy-nilly, as you may be sabotaging yourself without realizing it. You have already learned about the importance of being open to *receiving*, so here are two more.

Rule #1: Do not allow anyone, or any organization or institution, for that matter, to dictate when, how, why, and the quantity in which you give.

Rule #2: Don't give things to people just because they ask for it, especially in the case of money.

The purpose of these rules is to help you think and make decisions for yourself, because when you refuse to do so, you allow other people to determine things for you rather than living life on your terms. When it comes to giving, the onus is on you to understand the following:

Giving is best done freely and joyously for it to be effective. When you violate either rule by giving in the scenarios as described, you are, more than likely, doing so out of a sense of duty and obligation-which will not move your heart, since you really do not feel that you have a choice in the matter. Also, you may not fully agree with the manner in which your giving was suggested.

For example, I have some friends who give faithfully to their religious institutions. Yet they resent the fact that there is a certain expectation of them to do so. There are still others who are in favour of the work done by social charities, but do not like the constant solicitation to make donations. Does this sound like giving joyously and freely to you? When that joyous feeling is lacking, your act of giving becomes counterproductive and nothing will come back to you. Now you know the reason why you may have been *giving* all your life, but the abundance train has not been stopping at your station. There is a high probability that you were violating the rules without even knowing it. When you find joy in *Giving*, go for it!

Highest Form of *Giving*

I believe that the highest form of *Giving* is to provide a product or service that improves the lives of others, regardless of whether it is for profit or not. One is not more ideal than the other. Also, service comes in many forms, whether you are an employee, volunteer, musician, doctor, mentor, coach, or a businessperson. You get to decide according to your preference, as long as what you are providing adds value to other people's lives. You succeed quickest by helping others succeed. If you would like to experience abundance in your life, put service first and the rest will take care of itself. Let me tell you a story to prove this point.

I have a friend who is a mentor and counselor. He is a keen listener and, when solicited, he always takes time out to offer advice, whatever your issue. This guy is always looking out for the interest of others. When I met him ten years ago, I was still new to Ottawa and he gave me a crash course on survival in the current environment in which I had found myself. He especially gave me some insights as to navigating the corporate world with its various forms of office politics and the like. I was one of many people he mentored.

One day, I received a call from him while I was in a meeting at work. He left a voice message, letting me know that he needed some cash right away due to an emergency. Immediately, I excused myself from this important meeting and went to assist my friend. After I arrived at his office and gave him the cash, seven other people pulled up to assist him as well.

See, he was not sure if he would have reached me (due to my busy schedule) so he made calls to seven others as a result of the severity of his issue. So, up walked the other seven individuals with cash in hand. I looked at him and told him that he is the Richest Man in Canada. He received eight times the amount he needed.

The moral of the story is that my friend's continuous, never-ending giving of his time to share his wisdom, adds value to us. His contributions have influenced us and enriched our development as human beings. How else do you explain eight people dropping whatever we were doing and ignoring all repercussions (all of us with jobs and responsibility) in order to come to this gentleman's aid? This man has bettered the lives of many. As a result, he will always be taken care of. Always!

Caution! Before I end this chapter, I must warn you about a certain practice of which many people are guilty. When it comes to attracting more abundance in your life, resist the urge of trying to get something for nothing. You cannot outsmart the Universe. You must give in order to receive, because the quality of what you give is what you will certainly receive.

Also, you must pay the price in full and in advance. You will achieve your dreams and desires only after you have paid the price, in the form of continuous, persistent action. Too many people are attracted to the short-cuts of life. Don't be one of them! You have heard that there is no such thing as a free lunch, so if you are enjoying a free lunch, it is evidence of an exchange!

The nuances of *Giving* have been revealed to you. We have dispelled the myth that states it is far better to give than to receive. And finally, you were told about the highest form of *Giving*. Now what?

Action Exercises

1. Practice giving your time and resources to someone or an organization of your choosing. Remember that the choice has to be yours for you to feel good about it.

2. When giving, do so without hesitation or reservation of any kind. This depicts your belief in the abundance of the Universe. And your belief in abundance will lead you to abundance.

As I say quite often, you can be skeptical of this information, but skepticism will not serve any purpose for you. However, if you decide to be successful and achieve anything you imagine, then you will find that applying the information available to you in this book will be to your benefit.

It is not that which we wish for that comes back to us,
but that which we give.

~ Napoleon Hill

Chapter 7

Forgiveness: The Liberator

The unhappiest of mortals are those who insist on reliving the past.

~ Dr. Maxwell Maltz

VERY FEW SUCCESS books, if any, talk about the pivotal role the act of *Forgiveness* plays in contributing to your success. Maybe the various authors did not deem it worthy of note, or perhaps (giving them the benefit of the doubt) they just assumed that you already knew of this life success hack.

Your ability to truly forgive others – and yourself – for past transgressions in thought and deed is essential to activate your positive flow of energy. As this chapter progresses, you will see how the link between forgiveness and success reveals how this positive flow of energy creates a better You.

The theme throughout this book is how to use simple action to achieve anything you imagine. It is challenging enough to act when in a positive frame of mind, and even more challenging to act when in a state of negativity with a clouded and toxic mind. To act impactfully, you must be aligned with positive energy.

Now, when you are able to forgive others, you clear out all the mental crap that has been holding you back all this time and this action makes room for positivity. Let me interject here and say this: If you think holding grudges does not affect your day-to-day performance, think again. It is taking up valuable space in your mind and utilizing energy that you could be using for constructive purposes.

When you forgive, people and / or events no longer have control over you because you have released the chains that were holding your mind in bondage. You will find that this act of forgiveness allows your positive energy to flow freely, which then activates your natural creative state, enabling you to think about, and to design, the life you have always imagined living.

To summarize in a simpler manner, *Forgiveness* eradicates your grievances so that you can use your time focusing on your goals. Forgiving others helps you to move forward with your life. Vendettas be damned! When I consciously decided to go after my dreams, I made a list of all the people who I *felt* had wronged me, as well as those whom I had wronged. For the latter group – once I had their contact information – I called them up and asked each and every one of them to forgive me for the things I either said about them or did to them.

I must admit that I was rather embarrassed during some of those calls, because having to eat humble pie and throwing myself at the mercy of another person is not the greatest feeling in the world. But it needed to be done. See, in my mind, I needed to make peace with these people or else *something* would always be holding me back. And I could not afford this limitation because I was intent on being on my journey to super success.

Now for the other group – the ones who had wronged me – I simply forgave them and wiped the slate clean. Wow! That was a liberating feeling. Let me digress to state that it does not necessarily mean that you and the other person will be buddy-buddy again after forgiveness takes place. The point is that the slate has to be wiped clean.

Anyway, after engaging in both exercises, of seeking forgiveness and forgiving, it was as though I experienced instant transformation. New ideas were rushing into my mind regarding old problems. I felt lighter. It was as if I had hit the reset button. A new beginning was underway, all because I chose to forgive others, as well as asking others to forgive me.

Natural Urge

Hear me and hear me well. If you are serious about success, avoid getting even. Consider the cost of engaging yourself in this destructive emotional act. Your desire to get even will only hurt you, because it drains your energy and distracts you from focusing on your goals. Success is the result of consistent, persistent and efficient effort. And if you are busy devising and plotting ways to take revenge, you are doing so at your own expense – unless your true dream is to permanently be seeking revenge on someone for something they have done – in which case, I cannot help you. So, given what you now know, is getting back at someone worth the effort?

The Liberator

So, what am I alluding to when I coin *Forgiveness* as **The Liberator**? Your ability and willingness to forgive removes the shackles of the **Triple Rs**. And what are the **Triple Rs**? Allow me to introduce you to **Resentment, Remorse** and **Regret**. They each have tremendous power in keeping you stuck and creating havoc in your life. Release yourself! Be free!

Resentment

Resentment affects health, and maintaining good health is paramount in the pursuit of your dreams. You can dream all you want, but if your health is deplorable, you will either fall short of achieving your dreams, or not even enjoying the journey. Simply, being full of resentment makes it virtually impossible to be happy and eventually leads to self-pity which, in my opinion, is a pathetic emotional state.

Chronic resentment creates hypertension and heart trouble by continuously aiming resentment toward someone or something. Yet, you may be determined to engage in this destructive attitude. *But I can't forgive him. I just can't let go of what was done to me.* OK! Know, though, that you are a ticking time-bomb, with the only casualty being you! And how will you achieve anything you imagine (other than more ill-health) when you are in terrible health, immobilized by resentment, or, worse, dead?

I am sure you have heard that when you refuse to forgive, you are giving the transgressor power over you. Symptoms of resentment include lack of sleep and loss of appetite, but here is the real tragedy: Harbouring resentment makes it difficult (even impossible) for you to think of yourself as a self-reliant, independent, confident individual, all of which are required for you to be successful. Resentment is synonymous with failure, being inconsistent with goal-setting and, subsequently, goal-getting.

Newsflash! Truly successful people do not hold grudges, as they know the havoc this creates for their health. Also, where you focus your attention determines your emotional state and if you're fixated on being resentful, you are hindering your own personal performance toward your goals.

Remorse

Remorse provides the perfect excuse for us to give in and stay in the doldrums. We tell ourselves that we are unable to rise above sorrow, so we keep stewing and brooding over the event or situation that befell us. Ultimately, we stop living *actively* and with purpose when we allow ourselves to be overcome by grief. We go through the motions of day-to-day living with no inspiration or motivation. Living in this manner is not conducive to goal-attainment or dream-achievement.

Even though you cannot change what happened to you or to someone else, you can change your *perception* about what happened. This shift in outlook is key for changing your current circumstances and what is possible. If you missed what I just said, then you can forget about ever acting on your dreams. Let me give you an example. What I am about to share may appear to be cold and insensitive. However, my aim is not to offend anyone. I am merely providing another perspective. So here goes.

When my younger brother (eleven years my junior) passed away, some members of my family chose to wallow in endless sorrow. Although experiencing sadness and pain as well, I used my brother's death as a source of inspiration to better myself. See, as my brother was dying, I realized that life is waaaaaaay too short, and if I was going to have an impact on the lives of others before

I take that particular ride as my brother was then taking, I had to get my act together, and get it together at that very moment. Plus, my brother was so full of wisdom that I felt: who better for me to emulate than him? Mind you, he was only thirteen years old at the time of his death.

My decision enabled me to get back on track with my life with a renewed sense of purpose. In the process, as time passed, my sadness and pain lessened. Meanwhile, some family members cannot get over the event, even to this day, and continue to allow themselves to still be stricken by grief. At times, it appears as though they are upset with life and looking for something to blame – although I am not sure who or what is to be blamed in this instance. And to the point I was making earlier, they are now just going through the motions of living.

The experience of losing my brother taught me some additional lessons. For one, to return to the normal course of life as soon as possible. If I were to allow remorse to crystallize, it would stay with me for a long time. For another, I chose to get active, both constructively and productively. This form of action is highly emphasized because experiencing so-called bad situations is not an excuse for you to get involved in escapism and destructive behaviour in order to mask the pain. Cry and get help when you need to but returning to normalcy as soon as possible is important.

I have used the example of my brother's death, though for you, what is it that has caused you to experience deep pain? For instance, you may be going through a painful divorce. The point is that remorse can be conquered but, in order to overcome it, you have to make the decision – another form of action-taking – to do so.

Start by forgiving the person or event (yes, you can forgive the event, like I did in the case of my brother's death) that caused you hurt. With a lighter heart and a clearer mind, you will be able to resume your journey toward your dreams. Remember also that you can use the sad event as a means of inspiration along the way.

Regret

Living with regret is very common. Regrets are usually based on things not done. And for whatever reason (guilt, probably) people cannot seem to get over regret. For instance, my father keeps lamenting his regret about not providing any support (financially and otherwise) when I was a child. He regrets not being in my life during my formative years and even part of my adulthood.

I told him several years ago that living in the past serves us both no purpose and that all I cared about was having a wonderful relationship together going forward. I forgave him, but the major stumbling block is that he seems unwilling to forgive himself. The result is that he is presently sabotaging himself from achieving his goal of having a better relationship with me because of his choice to keep living with regret.

Listen! Do not be like my dad and sooooo many others. Choose to stop living in the past. Living in the past does not do you any good unless it is to identify the lesson in the unpleasant experience and to learn from it. The important thing is to focus on your *present* direction and your *present* goal. Notice the word *present* is emphasized, as this is the only place where you can create better circumstances – and in the process, a better life – for yourself.

You cannot create in the past and you certainly cannot create in the future because the future has not yet arrived. Successful people know that success is in the ability to rise in the face of so-called failure, and that this is not possible when they are living in the past. When you live in the past, your past becomes your present, thus preventing you from moving forward into your fresh future (new present).

Living with regrets sometimes becomes a badge of honour. Maybe you are looking for sympathy, or maybe you think you have to pay an eternal penance for something from your past. Either way, what good is this doing for you? There are times when your challenge will be to forgive yourself. This is not an easy task. Forgive yourself and carry on with going after what you truly desire.

So far, my dad fails to grasp this concept of regret. Hence, he is stuck at the same place, lamenting the same thing. I can tell you this much: he will not get any sympathy from me. Why? My desire is to have a great relationship with him... not to be a carded member of his pity party.

The Take-Away

By now, you will have seen and understood the connection between *Forgiveness* and *Success*. I am asked all the time what the two have to do with each other. I assure you, they are not mutually exclusive. The following statement sums up what I have repeatedly stated in this book, and this repetition is for a reason (yes, there is a method to my madness): Being successful requires you to become a better version of yourself. And you cannot be a better YOU if you are unable to forgive.

See how it all works? See how everything seems to be all connected and intertwined in a circle? That is because it is. Give *Forgiveness* a chance. You will be happier for it. Forgiveness frees (liberates) you from bondage and renews your energy so that you can go after the things that truly matter to you, thus achieving success in the process.

Action Exercises

1. Make a list of the people who have transgressed against you. Resolve to forgive them and then wipe the slate clean.

2. If you are the transgressor, ask for forgiveness from those who were hurt by you.

3. Make a decision to live in the present, thus leaving your past behind. This resolve will dissolve resentment, remorse and regret.

4. Feel the weight being lifted from your shoulders. Doesn't this feel amazing? Yes, it does. You have just opened up your flow of energy.

Forgiveness is the fragrance that the violet sheds on the heel that has crushed it.

~ Mark Twain

SECTION 3

The Pitfalls

Chapter 8

Fear: The Deadly Poison

*Fear and worry steal the effectiveness of
human endeavour and happiness.*

~ Ralph Waldo Trine

WE ALL HAVE fear of some kind or another. It is said that fear is responsible for people's failures more than anything else. In the words of David J. Schwartz, Ph.D., "Fear is success enemy number one... action cures fear." Fear prevents people from starting new relationships and new businesses, from standing up for themselves, from investing and taking risks, from capitalizing on opportunities and from taking leadership roles.

Whatever the desire, people allow fear to be their stumbling block. Their minds are constantly scanning for what is wrong or what could go wrong in any situation. Simply stated, fear paralyzes them from doing what they truly want to do with their lives.

Life-Saving Fear

Before I go any further, I must acknowledge that there have been times when fear kept me alive. Like the time my mother told me not to have the school call at her place of employment to tell her I was in trouble. That made me a model student because my mom had a penchant for embarrassing her children in public. Another time she advised that if I was ever arrested by the cops, then too bad, so sad. I was not to waste my one phone call by contacting her.

Those particular fears kept me on the straight and very narrow. My mom was big on discipline and once you misbehaved, it was fair game. She constantly reminded me that she brought me into this world and she will gladly oblige by taking me out.

Another time when fear saved my life was when my grand-mother informed me that if I should get into a fight, to please make sure that I had won. She made it clear to me that if I came home and told her otherwise, she would give me an additional beating, as well as ceasing to provide food for me. According to her, why should she provide meals for a loser? Yes, you guessed correctly, she was my mother's mom.

Sorry to disappoint you, but life-saving fears are not the types of fear that I will be talking about. My examples are what I call strong motivations to get my act – wanted to use another word, but this is a kid-friendly book – together. The type of fear I am about to address is the crippling type that breeds doubt, apprehension and procrastination.

A Bad Habit

Fear is a habit. It is not natural, as most would like you to believe. Napoleon Hill describes fear as a "self-generating morass." We create our own quagmire with our fearful thoughts. Fear and its companion, worry, rob you of your happiness. This is true in all areas of your life. For years, I was terrified of dogs. In my early teens, I was bitten by a dog that I knew very well. Two decades later, it still had a profound effect on me. For example, when I would go rollerblading and see a dog, I would stop at least 100 yards away, and request that the dog be placed on a leash. It did not matter the type of dog. After a while, I quit rollerblading altogether. My fear of dogs prevented me from doing something I greatly enjoyed.

In the same manner, we allow the effects of fear to stop us dead in our tracks from pursuing our goals and dreams. We even resort to blaming our circumstances. Before I ventured into real estate development, I had a laundry list of circumstances as justification for not embarking upon the opportunity. How could I come up with the money for capital investment? Is the market for real estate strong at this time? What if things turned sour? What would my family think? Fear was my master. And it was stifling me. Which. Sucked. Big. Time.

Good News

Fortunately, I soon learned the solution for conquering and overcoming fear. Taking Action! No matter how small. So, I recommend that you, too, make a decision on the object of your desire and then immediately act upon it. The longer you hesitate or procrastinate, the larger and more magnified your fear becomes. To cure fear, you must act. And act now. Not tomorrow. Not when you get a pay raise. Not when you find the perfect partner. Now!

In the case of my fear of dogs, an opportunity arose where I was in very close proximity to two Dobermans. Instead of passing on the experience, I nervously decided to use the opportunity to overcome my fear. The result: in about two hours, I was much more comfortable in the presence of dogs. What a liberating feeling that was. I am not saying that I became Dr. Dolittle overnight, but I was not a nervous wreck any longer. From that point on, I feel more comfortable around canines.

I applied the same concept in my decision to get involved in real estate. Instead of worrying about *how* to come up with capital, I took inspired action. Before long, the money started to flow in for each project. Today, any time I sense fear creeping into my mind, I gather the pertinent and relevant information, make a decision and then follow through on it.

And if I am having trouble getting my act together, I have a particular friend who whips me into shape pretty quickly. Trust me; she is a true G.I. Jane. So, overcome fear by promptly taking action. Action eradicates anxiety and apprehension and activates hope. When you need help taking action, choose a mentor to help you work through your fears and move forward on your path.

According to Les Brown, motivational guru extraordinaire, "Too many people are not living their dreams because they are living their fears." And what are some of these fears? Well, I think they can be condensed and classified into two types: fear of failure and fear of ridicule.

Fear of Failure

Of the two types of fear, I was more tormented by fear of failure. I was terrified at the thought of falling flat on my face in the pursuit of my dream, until it dawned on me that each setback was a positive event in disguise. Instead of getting disheartened and down on myself, I flipped my mindset and decided that no matter what unfortunate event befell me, I would consider it to be one step closer to a breakthrough.

Maybe it was a coping mechanism, but I started looking at things with fresh eyes. I began to view my setbacks as vital to my growth. These events all contained a lesson that I had to learn. So, I got to learning. I searched for the lesson in each event and moved on. Life success hack: salvage something from every setback.

When you experience setbacks, rest assured they are helping to make you better. As Ben Arment, author of *Dream Year* so eloquently put it, "Your life is being equipped with exactly the kind of experiences your true dream requires." Rather than viewing your setbacks to be failures, consider them to be necessary. They are preparatory steps to the next level on your journey.

Some of my epic disasters have been the catalyst for my greatest triumphs. One event comes to mind. Over twenty years ago, I almost quit soccer before my career even got off the ground. I was coming up through the ranks and got my chance to play for my country's junior team. This was a huge deal, because it meant if I played well, I would be kept in the program and eventually be considered for the senior team, with the big boys.

And so, on that fateful night in April 1994, we played against one of the neighbouring countries and we received a beat-down of epic proportions. Guess who played in goal that night? Yep. Me. I was crushed. I stayed inside and cried for three months (yikes, talk about being in touch with your feelings) and vowed never to play soccer again.

After a conversation with my friend, G.I. Jane (who called me a few choice names), I challenged myself to find the lesson in my reaction to the defeat. And lo and behold, it dawned on me that I was embarking on a career of professional sports and would need to develop a thick skin. I was too fragile mentally and, if I wanted to play with the big boys, then I would have to put on my big boy pants.

Within the next 18 months, I became the first goalie to be named National Player of the Year, and at 19 years old, the youngest as well, a record that still remains today. My prior setback was the lever that catapulted me to the top. So, embrace your so-called failures. They are catalysts to assist you.

Fear of Ridicule

Come to think of it, fear of ridicule might affect people more than fear of failing. We are too concerned about what others might say when we go after our dreams. For some reason we are looking for permission or validation from others. From personal experience, let me tell you that the sooner you stop giving a crap about what other people think, the more time and energy you will have to do something worthwhile with your life. You will be closer to freedom.

Do not be concerned if people do not fully embrace or understand your dream. People's opinions are not a deal-breaker for you. You are a unique individual with unique desires, so only you can really understand and be in love with your dream. This is okay.

You only need your own approval. If people are busy criticizing and ridiculing you, it means that you are making real progress. As my grandfather would say, "dogs do not bark at parked cars." Tough analogy but, oh very true! So, do not concern yourself about people being skeptical or even doubtful. One day, things will become clearer to them. And if they are still confused, who cares?

This is why it is so important that you are passionate about your dream. When you are filled with passion and enthusiasm and totally believe in your dream, there is no time for the naysayers. Summon your inner strength! Remember, people do not like to leave their comfort zone. When they are ridiculing you, realize it is their way of attempting to keep you in the quagmire with them.

Since they themselves are not moving ahead and are feeling

inadequate, their goal is to make a mediocre person out of you. If you are having a hard time getting over criticism, think of it this way. You are playing the game of life, while your detractors are mere spectators. They are watching you move in the direction of your dream while they remain stagnant. How do you like them apples?

Action Exercises

1. Examine your list of fears. Find out where and how you acquired them. I am appealing to you to take this first step of identifying your fears to bring them into the light.

2. What actions are you putting off out of fear and what is fear costing you? Trust me when I say this: Fear costs you physically, emotionally and financially.

3. Take the necessary actions to overcome them. Get help if need be. Fear is the chief reason for poverty, failure and misery. Those who master fear place themselves on the path of successful achievement in any endeavour.

4. Most importantly, I recommend staying away from the what-if experts. These are the type who quiz (sorry, interrogate) you about all the things that could go wrong. This recommendation will advance you speedily. The result will be rewarding. Do you realize the majority of things we worry about, never happen?

5. Always take constructive and productive action pertaining to your dreams and goals. Action makes you feel positive and in control. You will be glad you took action.

As you eradicate fear from your mind, confidence takes its place. Action strengthens confidence and confidence is a key ingredient to success. While overnight success is not guaranteed, your habit of daily action is a life success hack that will bring you success over time. Action causes momentum. Momentum breeds more action. And action combined with momentum ultimately leads to success. You are on your way!

*Life shrinks or expands in proportion
to one's courage.*

~ Anais Nin

Chapter 9

Excuses: The Disease of the Mind

Most people let conditions control their attitudes instead of using their attitudes to control conditions.

~ Allan Bellamy

EXCUSES ARE SELF-DEFEATING thoughts. As stated by Alexander Pope, "An excuse is worse and more terrible than a lie, for an excuse is a lie guarded." The problem with excuses is that they appear to have credence and people use them to justify their reasons for not doing anything worthwhile with their lives. Take a look at the following common excuses and ask yourself if you suffer from any one of these mental diseases. Yes, you heard me! An excuse is a mental disease, which festers and expands.

Kids

"I have kids" is a major excuse! Most people will tell you that they cannot take action on their dreams because they have children or a family to support. Let me cut to the chase. What you are basically saying is that your children are the reason for you settling for mediocrity. You are blaming them for your sorry state of a life.

Stop blaming your children. Has it ever occurred to you that, as a parent, you owe it to your children to demonstrate to them how it is possible for them to live fully and freely? You can teach them how to persevere and chase their dreams. Who better for them to emulate than you? And what better way to inspire them than by living fully and freely yourself?

You are probably thinking that you are living freely now. Let me tell you something. If you are doing something in your life just to pay the bills and make ends meet or doing something that you are not truly passionate about, chances are that you are not living freely and fully. Instead of living, you are merely *surviving*. This type of life lacks vitality and enthusiasm and for your children it offers limited perspective on what is possible.

As a father, I believe it is my duty to live a life of vigour and prosperity for my daughter to see that people can achieve anything they imagine when they have a burning desire and put in the necessary work. No circumstance or obstacle will prevent me from going after my dreams. And what better way to have a meaningful influence on my daughter than for her to observe how I overcome obstacles on my way to my dream? I figure that this will encourage her to recognize unfavourable things as part of the journey, so then what would be her excuse? Keep this life success hack top of mind when you need to inspire or motivate your kids.

Lack of Money

The proponents of the "I have no money!" excuse will tell you that you need money to make money. Actually, thoughts and ideas make money. However, more often the issue is one of priorities.

It is amazing what people spend money on. We have the necessary funds to purchase that nice big screen television or the latest gadgets from Apple and Samsung. Or we spend a significant sum on purchasing items that are not good for our health. (Things such as cigarettes come to mind, but hey, I am not judging, I am just commenting on this lifestyle.) These same people will look me straight in the eye and tell me that they cannot afford to pay for a seminar or a course that would aid with their personal development.

Further, I have heard the justification for this lack-of-money excuse that the items were bought on credit, and that there is no extra cash to invest in personal development. As irrational as that sounds, people defend this excuse vehemently. However, hear this: If you are willing to put yourself in debt to obtain depreciating items, then you should be willing to borrow the funds in order to invest in yourself. Borrow it. Beg it. Do not be ashamed. After all, you were not ashamed to buy that lovely iPad with money that you didn't have in the first place.

A lack of money should never be a reason for you not to chase your dreams. As a matter of fact, it should be entirely the opposite, whereby you go after your dreams so that you never ever have to experience a lack of money again. Stop selling yourself short. Money is all around you, and you will notice it when you choose life-serving habits.

Time

Just as with money, the excuse about time comes down to priority management. When people say they cannot find time, the question arises, "What are you unwilling to give up?" Maybe it is an unwillingness to give up watching the latest prime time programs, thereby insisting on "Keeping up with the Kardashians." Or it could be a refusal to give up any one of many unproductive hobbies, such as socializing on Facebook. We seldom stop to think that this time could be spent writing that business plan that we have been procrastinating on. Our time could be spent doing something / anything that helps us to become a little better as people rather than wasting precious moments on mere distractions.

A friend once told me that he struggled to find time to work on his dream of starting a food catering business. His reasons seemed legitimate as he has a wife and children. But he was determined to change things, so he discussed the issue with his family and they came to an agreement. The children, being teenage kids, were going to be responsible for getting to and from their various activities. This would free him from having to constantly be a chauffeur, so he could use that time to work on his goals.

Additionally, both he and his wife realized that lots of time was spent associating with their respective in-laws, something that neither of them really enjoyed. So, they decided to change things in this part of their schedule, too. By taking stock of how he spent his time, my friend was able to replace his unproductive activities with motivation-building actions in the direction of his dreams. Like my friend, I bet you have comparable choices you can make to remove unproductive activities from your schedule that will create momentum.

Age

I hear this all the time, "I am too old." To illustrate the fallacy of this excuse, consider this chain of thought. Most people believe 20 years is a long time. So, if you are 60 years old now, and let's say you have another 20 years to live, my question is: what are you going to do during these 20 *long* years? Are you going to just live in sheer boredom and regret until death rescues you from your mundane life? I hope not. Get excited! Get enthusiastic! In fact, you might have an advantage over others, based on the life experiences you have accumulated over the years.

Within you is the ability and power, at any stage of your life, to do anything you imagine. This power becomes available to you as soon as you alter your beliefs about your age and capabilities. Don't believe me? Remember Colonel Sanders, yes, the good ol' founder of KFC? He was in his mid-sixties when his business idea took off. C.S. Lewis was correct when he stated that "You are never too old to set another goal or to dream another dream." You are the age you are, and your thoughts and ideas are ageless.

One guy who I know is in the process of re-inventing his business. He owns a print shop and wants to take advantage of social media to expand his business. And why is this extraordinary? He is seventy-two. Most people at that age are looking to wrap things up. But not this particular guy. He is looking to ramp things up.

Lack of Education

Some of us simply think that we are not smart enough. We do not know all the *hows*. Newsflash! Einstein was no Einstein. He considered himself limited as a mathematician so he enlisted the assistance of his colleagues to help him test his theories. Also, I am sure by now that you have heard about Henry Ford. He had little to no formal education. Yet, he became the richest man in the world at one point. He did not let his lack of formal education prevent him from making something of himself.

The point is threefold: first, Einstein and Ford did not let limitation stop them; secondly, there are others who can assist us with the *hows;* and thirdly, it is our determination to accomplish our goal that allows the *hows* to be revealed along the way.

In each of us lives vast intelligence that is beyond traditional earthly education. Our attitude guides our thinking through education into the emergence of our ideas. Our ideas about what we would like to become or to accomplish are evidence of inner genius. Passion, not education, activates genius. What are you passionate about?

Not Good Enough (Unworthy)

Let me be blunt. If you think you are not good enough or not worthy of success, you lack self-esteem. Plain and simple! I am here to tell you that since you are a part of this Universe, you are worthy. Full stop. Period! This excuse of being not good enough keeps you discouraged and while it may appear to protect you, all it does is hold you back from taking action.

What makes you think other people are worthy of success more than you are? Where did you get this self-defeating belief? I suspect you feel this way because of the opinions of others. The only person who can determine your worthiness is You. Stop sabotaging yourself. You already have what it takes to be all you can be. A little belief goes a long way.

It's Too Late to Act

Stop procrastinating! It's never too late to do anything. Does Apple ever contact you and tell you it is too late to sell you one of its products? Or do you hear from your government, saying it is too late to send you that tax bill from five years ago? If it is not too late for them, it is not too late for you. The best time to do anything is right now. So, get to it. Don't wait until everything is perfect before you act.

The Take-Away

Excuses hold you back you from achieving results. They explain the difference between the person who is going somewhere and the individual who is stuck in mediocrity. When you think about it, you realize that both unsuccessful and successful people alike could make excuses, right? The only thing standing between you being unsuccessful and successful is an excuse. Remember that your circumstances do not make you; they reveal you. Never give in to circumstances. Instead, use them as levers to catapult you in the direction you would like to go. I was told a long time ago that those who have excuses never have results and those who have results, do not need excuses. Which side are you on? Only You can decide where you want to be.

Action Exercises

1. Analyze the excuses you employ, and what it is costing you to employ them. Make sure you are fully aware of them. Do not judge yourself. Just observe objectively.

2. Ask yourself the following about your excuses:

    • Where did they originate?

    • Were they passed on to me from others?

    • Are they presently serving me in a positive manner?

3. Insert into your mind new and constructive thoughts, such as, *I can do that thing... I can have that thing... I can live with purpose and direction...* Over time, excuses will become a thing of the past.

Never let the odds keep you from pursuing what you know in your heart you were meant to do.

~ Satchel Paige

Chapter 10

Procrastination: The Master Thief

"Going to do it" never gets anyone anywhere.

~ Julia Seton

SOMEDAY! ONE DAY! When the time is right! When my circumstances change! As soon as I get around to it! Do these word and phrases sound familiar? I bet they do. The culprit who is responsible for these utterances is certainly not your friend. He lulls you into a false sense of comfort and security, only for you to awaken one day (if ever at all) with a tremendous case of feeling overwhelmed with shattered dreams. I now introduce you to him. His name is Procrastination, and he is a master thief.

The Master Thief in Action

Procrastination is a crafty and tricky little fellow. He carries out his work in a very subtle manner. You are not aware of his effects and influence until it is too late. For example, Procrastination robs you of opportunities by making you indecisive. In other words, he will not directly take opportunities from the palm of your hand. Instead, he lets you voluntarily throw them away.

Let me break it down. You may be walking around claiming that your life sucks and that you cannot catch a break. However, the truth of the matter is that opportunity exists all around you, yet you do nothing, even when it is staring you in the face. Consider this scenario. Let's say you are a person who needs to know all the information inside and out before you act upon anything. And no matter how much information you receive, you still require more.

You also need to see what everyone else is doing before you get a move on things. You jump back and forth, trying to decipher what you should do. You make a decision today and change your mind tomorrow. And this behaviour continues. By the time you are ready to act, the train has left the station. You are now standing there whining about life being unfair while waiting for someone to throw you a pity party with a banner stating Life Sucks. No. You suck! You were being an indecisive basket case who threw away an opportunity.

It Helps to Be Decisive

Indecision, a by-product of Procrastination, is a major weakness for many of us. If you are indecisive, you are doomed to failure. Let that swim around in your head for a while.

The number of times I encounter indecisive people is unbelievable. Most of them approach me about investing in real estate. They request all kinds of information, from the relevant to the absurd. The end result is usually the same. Their common refrain is "I need some more information, then I will get back to you about my decision." One guy had me questioning my sanity. In reality, he was never going to act on anything I suggested.

Author Napoleon Hill states, "A man of decision cannot be stopped." Alternatively, a man of indecision cannot be started. Success comes from decisiveness and course correction, rather than long delays and Procrastination. If you do not act upon opportunity, you are a procrastinator. Chances are that you are a fearmonger as well. Stop fooling yourself. There is a difference between doing due diligence and procrastinating.

No Judgement Here

Far be it from me to be passing judgement on you for succumbing to Procrastination. There are times when his tentacles grab a hold on me as well. For instance, several years ago, when I set a goal to begin writing to document my life's journey, I did everything other than what I had planned to do, which was writing.

By the way, this is another ploy Procrastination plays on you. He makes you engage in all types of activities except those that advance you towards your dreams and goals. And worse, you are convinced these menial and unproductive activities are essential tasks to be carried out prior to the main event, or the main course, so to speak. Whether that is checking emails while you could be preparing your thesis or posting on social media while your manager is waiting for that briefing note you planned to provide to her first thing in the morning.

My excuse as it pertains to writing was that I needed to do research. (Not sure why I needed to research my life's journey, since I am the one living said life.) The irony was that no amount of research was enough for me. The result: After three years, I did not have one solitary word written or typed. During all this time, Procrastination had me believe that I was doing what was necessary before the actual writing began. I was doing the groundwork; laying the foundation. Yeah, right. The truth is, I Sucked. Does this sound familiar to you?

Take Heed

I can tell you without hesitation that Procrastination is one of the most destructive habits there is. It is also one of the most popular forms of self-sabotage because it is so easy to do. It does not take any great effort. How many times have you ignored working on your goals in order to catch a movie with your buddies, or go shopping with your girlfriends? And this is not just something that happens once in a while. It is a familiar pattern. And how many times, when all is said and done, do you find yourself in a worse position or in a worse state of mind regarding your situation? You now have a laundry list of tasks, and nothing that depicts progress toward your dream of being a famous movie star.

Employ some self-discipline. You cannot afford to invite Procrastination into the mix when it comes to your goals and dreams. Be determined! Your job is to take inspired action to transform this habit that leads to nowhere into a habit that leads you to anywhere you imagine. You will reap the benefit of your discipline and win in life through your constructive and productive action.

Procrastination knows that even the most practical and sound plans are useless if they are not expressed in action. Instead of waiting for *someday*, or *one day*, or *when I get my promotion at work,* why not act now? I read somewhere that the word *now* is the magic word for success, which means that *tomorrow, next week, later, sometime* and *someday* are synonymous with the failure word – *never.*

I get accused of wanting everything done right away. I am told that I am impatient. Maybe this is true. But procrastinating is like public drunkenness. It feels good at the time and people love to revel in it. Yet we are surprised when life passes us by, leaving us with most of our desires unfulfilled.

Full Circle

Procrastination steals your dreams, your aspirations and, worse of all, your time. All while baiting you into a false sense of security. You think you are in control, while Procrastination, that little fellow, is the puppet master. I beseech you, please avoid Procrastination in all its forms. Each day, do all you can do so that you are closer to achieving your dream. I am not advising that you attempt to do the greatest possible number of things in the shortest possible time. This is not a race. Do not try to do a week's work in one day.

It is not the number of things you do. It is the number of right things that you do and the priority sequence in which they are done. Every act you perform must be efficient. If you adhere to what I am telling you, Procrastination does not have a chance to build a relationship with you. You will already be on your way before he even whispers your name.

Before I go any further though, do you believe me? Let me call out the procrastinator in you, that part of you who is still waiting until something changes in your life, or for your situation to improve. If you are waiting for the perfect set of conditions, you will wait forever. Do not wait until things are ideal in your life before you are willing to take action. Hello! Wake up! Your circumstances will never be ideal unless you make them so. You are responsible for creating whatever changes you want in your life. No one is coming over the hill to rescue you.

If you are ready for your circumstances to change, get up and get going. The action you take does not have to be enormous. Just take some steps to get things moving forward. Go as far as you can see and, when you get there, you will be able to see further. Taking action brings clarity to what you are aiming to achieve.

The Faces of Procrastination

Hello, Daydreamer in you. Thought I had forgotten about you, didn't you? You are the one with lots of wishes. *I wish this... I wish that...* Listen, stop the drifting. Yes, you are a drifter. And do not tell me that you are visualizing and shaping your life as you want it to be by creating a mental picture first. I agree that this practice is extremely important. However, without taking action, you are merely wishing for something as opposed to being willful about it.

The following scenario will help emphasize the point I am conveying. You dream about being a renowned chef. You visualize owning restaurants all over the world, where you receive many accolades and praise for your amazing dishes. You provide an exceptional and unforgettable dining experience. You can recite this dream to the minute detail, yet you have yet to take a cooking course. You have not held a pot in your life. And you have no intention of ever doing either of those things. You are in love with the outcome – being a master chef – and do not care about the work to get there. So, tell me, again: How are you going to become a world-class chef? Stop procrastinating. Go cook a meal.

Are you a Serial Learner? You are now on deck. You leave me scratching my head in disbelief at your thought process. Let me define you. You are the guy or gal who attends a bunch of seminars and workshops. You read all the self-help books. You *know* all the material. However, when I inquire if you have been applying any of the concepts that you were exposed to, your response is a big, fat "Not yet, because I am still learning."

I am not letting you off the hook. You already know the number one life success hack. Action. It is time to stop lying to yourself. The only thing you are learning is how to become better at procrastinating. That is all you are doing. This is similar to my excuse about needing to do research so I can begin documenting my own life. Has it ever dawned on you that you will learn more when you begin taking some sort of action, rather than merely reciting theoretical information about how things could be done?

Remember when I said earlier that success comes from decisiveness and course correction? Well, decide now to do something with all of this knowledge you have been acquiring since Noah built the Ark. You waited so long that the Ark was transformed into a steam liner.

The Universe has a funny way of letting us know the next steps, so do not concern yourself about figuring out the entire journey. If memory serves me correctly, it is an ancient Chinese proverb that observes: "A journey of a thousand miles begins with a single step." Do I need to tell you, yet again, to get to stepping?

Here are some tips on how to end Procrastination:

1. Hire a Mentor

A mentor is great because he or she is able to identify the times that you are most vulnerable with procrastinating. You may not be aware of these times, or what the real trigger is. Having a mentor will certainly assist you in this area. I don't want to hear about you not having money to hire a mentor. Money does not have to be a deal-breaker when it comes to going after your dreams and improving your life.

2. *Get an Accountability Partner*

If you are unable to afford a mentor at the moment, solicit the help of a good friend or co-worker who will hold you accountable. This has to be someone who terrifies you a bit. By *terrifies* I mean someone you respect so greatly that disappointing them would be a major issue for you. At the same time, this person will drag your carcass from pillar to post if you do not deliver on what you said you will do, and in the time that you said you will do it.

This will surely be obvious: do not... I repeat... do not have another procrastinator as your accountability partner. Both of you will just be teaching each other bad habits, which is counter-productive to what you are aiming to achieve.

3. *Take Inspired Action*

Dear Reader, when all is said and done, success boils down to taking inspired action in some way, shape or form. Even though you may not be the master of overcoming Procrastination as yet, you can still be taking one step at a time. Get started. Take small steps. And have fun along the way. By golly, just ACT!

Men of action are favoured by the Goddess of Good Luck.

~ George S. Clason

Chapter 11

Relationships: The Litmus Test

The most liberating of all thoughts is disregard for what other people think.

~ Dr. Maxwell Maltz

IMAGINE THE FOLLOWING: You have decided to go head-first in the direction of your dreams. Because of your enthusiasm and excitement, you tell your loved ones about your new journey. Instead of providing support and encouragement, they launch into highlighting everything that could go wrong. Some even attempt to talk you out of proceeding with your dream or goal.

Sound familiar? I remember the time I told my family that I was planning on relocating to Canada. In an attempt to relay the point in PG format, let us just say the overall reaction to my announcement was not the best. It did not matter to them that this had been a goal of mine since I was a child.

No Approval Needed

Your goal is your goal, not anyone else's. This is your life and only you can live it. There is a psychological tendency for others to feel threatened when anyone within their circle or group breaks away and does something different from tradition. The sooner you acknowledge that your family and friends may have self-defeating beliefs, and that you will not change their ways of thinking, the better. It is okay to break away from the pack. A lot of people are conformists and are more than willing to accept whatever miseries befall them than to take action on what they truly desire. They are usually living someone else's dream.

The intentions of your loved ones are likely self-serving, hence their reason for trying to talk you out of your dreams. Your decision to chase your dreams despite your circumstances, nullifies their list of justifications for not doing anything with their lives. To state it more bluntly, watching you chase your dreams can be extremely upsetting to someone who has spent their entire lifetime, so far, making excuses for why they, themselves, have yet to pursue their own dreams. When someone refuses to take responsibility for their own life, he or she cannot see the value in you wanting to take responsibility for your life. Misery, indeed, loves company.

Take Responsibility

Again, live your life according to your values and desires. This is where mentorship comes into play. Your job is to seek out people who will be supportive of you. Do not feel pressured into doing what is more comfortable for everyone else. Eventually, they will come to accept your decision and respect you greatly for it. Do not worry what your brother-in-law, Jesse, or Nancy, your neighbour two houses down, might think. The confidence you exude in spite of their objections and disapproval will make an impression on them and they may wonder how they can emulate you.

On a personal note, most of my friends and family felt I was crazy when they found out the manner in which I ventured into real estate investment. It was not the conventional way, but it was *my* way. I focused on trusting my gut. It was simply important to me that I took some sort of action. I gave over two hundred freaking thousand dollars to a total stranger to invest in real estate!! Two hundred thousand dollars (plus) that I had borrowed at the time, as I described earlier in this book. Talk about doing something radical. If you want to truly live a life you have never lived, you have to do things you have never done. For me, it was about trusting my intuition and not doubting for the sake of doubting.

Two-Way Street

Now, let us take a look at things from a different angle, or through a different lens, as a good friend of mine likes to say. When you adopt changes in your life, it is not always your loved ones who are guilty of transgressing or trespassing. You may also be guilty of not being respectful to them. Remember, you have chosen *your* path, but do not expect everyone else to do what you are doing.

Just as you want your loved ones to respect your choices, you do well to refrain from attempting to convince them to undertake the same journey as you. It took me awhile to come to this realization and even longer to practice it. When I made the decision to pursue financial freedom, I spent my time talking with everyone who would listen, highlighting the perils of having a 9-to-5 job.

This was a big mistake. Not everyone has the desire to leave their jobs and do something of their own. Instead of being seen as an inspiration, some of my friends felt offended by my unsolicited opinions. The irony is that once I stopped focusing on convincing others to make the same decisions as I was making, it was precisely the moment that I began having a positive impact and influence on their lives. I was simply being myself.

Your Immediate Task

1. Be yourself at all times. Everyone has different wishes, desires and goals. The best way to influence someone is to be blissfully happy yourself. If someone requests your advice, respectfully offer it. Otherwise, let others grow and develop as they see fit. Your job is not to convince them to follow you. Do not be the resident expert on everything life. People are free to do whatever makes them happy.

2. Be prepared that close association with your loved ones may diminish over time, due to the fact that their thought process is no longer aligned to your own. Whereas they might be doing just enough to get by, you are focusing on maximizing your potential. You cannot change your blood relatives, but you can reduce the amount of time you spend around those who are thinking small.

3. You may also want to get some new friends while you are at it, in the event your current ones are dream-killers. For your most intimate daily associates, select those who are in sympathy with your goals and dreams. In other words, hang around people who have a vested interest in your success. These are the people who cheer

you on. Or they inspire you. There is a direct relationship between one's environment and one's mental attitude. Hang around quitters and you will become a quitter. Spend the majority of your time around losers, and you will become a loser. Make sure that every one of your associates is a positive influence. Birds of a feather do indeed flock together. Soar high together!

It is a fact that while many people love the so-called security and safety in popular thinking, progress always requires change. The dynamics of your relationships with others in your circle may shift. You can continue to love and serve them, for service is the true measure of success. However, find a respectful way to limit the influence that Negative Nellies have on you. If you are able to do this, you will have passed a test that has caused many to stumble and fall.

Work on you before you concern yourself with others. People change when they want to and not when you want them to.

~ Larry Winget

Chapter 12

Money: The Falsely Accused

You cannot attract what you criticize.

~ Joseph Murphy

I HAVE SOME questions for you. Other than the devil, can you name one other thing that has a worse reputation than that of money? Do you view money (or the love of it) as the root of all evil? Money has always been blamed for the perils of the world. You might have issues with money right now. And I can bet it is being held responsible for you not being able to acquire some of the things you want in your life.

Here is the thing. You are not alone. Most people hold negative views of money. I will tell you the bad news in a bit, but first I would like to share with you about my upbringing as it pertains to the idea of money. Chances are you had a similar experience.

The Usual Suspect

As a kid, I was raised to believe that money was the cause of most, if not all, of the bad things happening in the world. It was always the rich versus the poor – those who had it, versus those who didn't. And because we were on the *have not* side, we were automatically enemies with those who had money. Money was blamed for crimes too. No one bothered to realize that it was greed and the lack of love and respect for others that were the real culprits.

Apparently, money was responsible for causing people to become *different* as well. By this I mean good people became heartless, filthy individuals the moment they acquired some money. As such, I grew up believing it was immoral for anyone to have lots of money. In my mind, the world would be better off without money-loving scumbags.

Critical Observation

Along the way, I observed how people who condemn and rebuke money were the same ones who prayed fervently for it to pay them a visit. This seemed contradictory but I dared not point out the hypocrisy. For instance, people will pray for money to buy food, or to help take care of a loved one who is sick. At the same time, they continue holding strong beliefs that money is a bad thing. Then I started thinking to myself, *If money is such a bad thing, then why were they requesting its appearance? Were they not just inviting trouble into their lives?*

In any event, things got more and more difficult for our family. Money continued its hide-and-seek act. But why was money being so elusive when I was growing up? Similarly, if that is your experience now, do you wonder why money is currently not paying you (pun intended) a visit?

Major Obstacle

Remember the bad news I promised to reveal to you earlier? Here it is. Your attitude and beliefs toward money are keeping you broke. Money is a sensitive fellow who steers clear of people who hold a negative viewpoint of him. And why shouldn't he? Would you continue to date someone who keeps belittling you?

Attracting money in your life is akin to courting someone to be your life partner. Okay, okay, before you think I am being melodramatic, let me explain. Men, do you believe a woman would consider you to be husband material if all you do is criticize and demean her? She will reject you faster than Usain Bolt running the 100-metre dash. You have a better chance of her hand in marriage if you tell her she is beautiful and that she is a smart and intelligent woman with whom you are deeply in love. In other words, compliment her and show her your Appreciation that she is in your life.

Time to Re-program

The same concept applies in your relationship with money. Yes, it is a relationship, so be mindful. Treat this relationship like any other important relationship. You want it. You nurture it. You cherish it. You love it (yes, *LOVE* it). And do not be ashamed of loving it either. You put effort into it. You express Gratitude for its existence.

By doing all these things, you will be paving the way for money to flow freely and joyfully into your life. Author Joseph Murphy summed it up best in his book, *The Power of the Subconscious Mind*. He states, "You cannot attract what you criticize. You lose what you condemn."

After reading all of these inspiring thoughts, are you still trying to figure out why money always seems to elude you like the Road Runner eluding the Coyote? Your negative feelings and beliefs regarding money are the issue. You are a money-repellent. And you are hanging around other broke, money-repellents. You are the cause of your own demise. Let me explain.

Money is not a scarce resource, as you may be apt to believe. It is always available for you to receive. But you must allow it into your experience. You hold it away from your life when you are criticizing it. Or condemning it. Or thinking it is filthy. Or believing that others will despise you for having it.

Instead, think about how money will serve and enrich your life and the lives of those closest to you. This will help you develop a more positive perception of money, bringing you into vibrational alignment with it. Once in vibrational alignment, you will notice money flowing freely through your life, just like the air you breathe, which is always present when you need it. If your experience and belief is that you are struggling to make ends meet, I strongly suggest you read the last two paragraphs a few more times.

Your View of Others

Do you subconsciously despise the wealthy? Do you think that they have more than they need? Again, if the answer is *yes*, you are blocking and preventing money from flowing for you. When we resent other people's wealth, we are essentially telling money to stay away. This is because we subconsciously attach a negative stigma to people who have (what we consider to be) tons of money, and we cannot attract what we criticize or what we condemn. Also, take note that money is not responsible for people's behaviour. Money is a magnifier, not a creator. So, if you were greedy before you had money, chances are you will be greedy after you acquire some money. In any case, your job is not to set the standards about how much money someone should be able to acquire. Nor should you be concerned about what they do with their money.

Stay with me, now. I can feel the slings and arrows coming my way. *How dare this guy defend those greedy people?* Just because they have lots of money does not mean you will have little or none. Again, money is not scarce. There is no lack of it. Think of money like acorns. Each year, squirrels gather acorns for the winter. But notice how Tommy Squirrel does not concern himself with how many acorns Joey Squirrel took? No, Tommy Squirrel simply collects what he needs and goes back to his home.

Also, and this is key. No matter how many acorns Joey Squirrel gathers (let us assume he gathers more than he needs – greedy little squirrel) do you notice that there is still an abundance of acorns available for other squirrels to enjoy to their heart's content? The same goes for money. Wait a minute! I can assure you that I am not a nut case who is speaking a bunch of nonsense. (Didn't think I heard you, did you?)

The Verdict

So, Derian, are you really telling me that I am solely responsible for the lack of money in my life? Yep, that is exactly what I am telling you.

And, are you saying that my current beliefs about money and regarding those who seem to have money in abundance, are the problem? Yes, again. That is what I am saying.

And, are you stating that when I form new, positive beliefs surrounding money that I will open the doorway to having money flowing more freely for me? Ding... Ding... Ding. You just won the grand prize. YES!! That is what I am stating!

My life experiences have provided me with considerable evidence of this fact. Since I changed my attitude and beliefs about money and regarding those who possess lots of it, money has followed me like a fairy godmother. There have been situations when I needed to manifest huge sums of cash in a short time frame without knowing the source of income. And like magic, the money came in at just the right time.

Sometimes money seems to appear out of thin air. I am reminded of the time when my daughter came to reside with me in Canada. Given the circumstances under which she came, there was an immediate need of approximately fifty thousand dollars to take care of legal and medical fees. Money did not abandon me because I had been doing my part in building a positive relationship with it.

Listen, I know you are probably having a hard time coming to terms with what I am telling you. I once had a tough time accepting this information as well. However, take it at face value and try it out. The proof is in the application of the knowledge. If it does not work, you can go back to calling me a nut case.

As usual, I am leaving you with a few guidelines to help with your re-programming:

1. Change your beliefs and feelings regarding money.

Develop a positive attitude towards money. Avoid being critical of it. Do your best to put money into context. That is, to never view it in isolation. Instead, think about how it will impact your life and the lives of those who are closest to you. Treat it as a good friend who is available to aid you at all times. What you believe about money will play a great role in how money plays out in your daily life.

2. Value rejoicing in the wealth of others.

This is not about worshipping anyone. It is about being happy for another person's success. Being happy for those who are manifesting great things into their lives is your way of acknowledging the abundance of the Universe. And when you acknowledge this abundance and express Appreciation, the Universe bestows gifts upon you. Just take my word for it.

3. Listen to what you say.

Speak of things as you desire them to be, rather than about how they are currently. When you dwell on dissatisfaction of how things are, you are moving away from vibrational alignment with abundance. In other words, constantly speaking of your money troubles will continue to give you just that: money troubles.

In wrapping up this chapter, it is my pleasure to let you in on a little secret while you are working on attracting more money into your life. Money is an excellent servant but a terrible master. It serves you better when it is working for you than when you are working for it. Life is one big paradox. Go figure!

Life is more important than money, but money is important for supporting life.

~ Robert Kiyosaki

SECTION 4

The Secrets

Chapter 13

Thoughts: The Secret Sauce

For as he thinketh in his heart, so is he.

~ Proverbs 23:7

LIKE A RAGING bull ready to charge the matador, I am flying out of the gates straight away on this one. Your success or lack thereof, depends on your thoughts – your mindset – which determines your actions. Ralph Waldo Emerson said that, "A man is what he thinks all day long." In other words, you become what you think about most. And so, if you think most about doing great things, you will achieve great things, thus becoming great in the process. If you think mostly mediocre thoughts – for example, having and doing just enough to get by – then you will live in mediocrity. Finally, if you do not think at all, then not much, if anything, can be done for you. Why? Simply put, if you think about *nothing* then you become nothing. I am not responsible for these laws, so do not get upset at me. I am just telling you how it works.

Thoughts of Escaping

As I have mentioned, I grew up in poverty (in the financial sense) on a little tropical island with faint hope that things would get better. However, in spite of the abject conditions, I began thinking about all the ways I could have a better life.

One of the first things I thought about was that I would attend the best school on the island: St. Joseph's Academy. This was an all-boys private high school. The students who attended St. Joseph's Academy were the sons of people from the so-called upper echelon of society – doctors, politicians, lawyers, and the like. I figured being a graduate of this prestigious institution would mean access to desirable employment, which would offer me the ability to earn more so that I could provide a better life for myself. Mind you, I did not have the foggiest idea of where the money would come from to pay the tuition. Many others had to give up their dream of attending the school of their choice because their parents could not afford the fees. My parents were no different.

Despite this, each day I thought about being enrolled at St. Joseph's Academy. I thought about excelling at this school, earning academic and athletic awards. I imagined the way my uniform would look on me, as well as the knapsack I would use to transport my books. These thoughts were doing something to me.

Thoughts Transformed into Beliefs

Here's the point. Your thoughts are the creative spark that will determine whether or not you chase your dreams. Prolonged thoughts become your belief pattern. And what you believe determines how you behave. When beliefs evolve into a deep conviction (a knowing-ness), you get a strong urge to act.

My dominant thought – having a better life – led me to believe that attending St. Joseph's Academy was the answer for me changing my circumstances. In each waking moment, I thought about attending this school and getting excellent grades. This repetition of thought led to the belief that I was going to accomplish the feat of attending St. Joseph's Academy. It was a done deal.

Remember what you were reading earlier about beliefs determining behaviour? Well, I began to act on my belief that I would attend that school. I disciplined myself and studied accordingly. I also researched various individuals who had attended, or who were presently attending that school. I became obsessed with that desire. It was all I could think about.

Things Falling into Place

Things just seemed to fall into place as the years went by. For instance, about three years later – I was then ten years old – my mom inquired about my interest in attending St. Joseph's Academy. She had never addressed this subject with me before. Soon thereafter, we learned that the school had relaxed its tuition policy. Tuition could now be paid with installments. This surely made it a bit more affordable for someone like me to attend.

A number of other events began happening as well. It was as if the stage was being set for me to accomplish my dream. What I did not know at that time, was that all of this was made possible because of my thoughts. As Claude Bristol rightly stated, "The secret of success lies not without, but within, the thoughts of man…

Man's thoughts make or break him." What about you? Are your thoughts making you or breaking you?

3 Key Principles

First key principle: Your belief is the force or power that leads to accomplishment. It is the motivating factor that will enable you to achieve your goal. Without belief in your goals or dreams, nothing will happen. If I did not truly believe that I would attend St. Joseph's Academy, then even though I was repeatedly telling myself that I would attend that school, my efforts would have been half-assed at best. My belief was the life success hack that set me in motion to act.

Second key principle: For thoughts to be of any positive and constructive assistance to you in achieving your goals, they must be frequent. More importantly, they must feel good when you are thinking them. So, to bring you back to the story of me attending the school of my choice, I did not only think about this once in a while. I thought about my dream frequently – over and over and over and over. And when I thought about it, I felt great. As a matter of fact, each time I thought about attending that school, it was as if I was attending St. Joseph's Academy at that very moment.

Lastly, notice that at no time at all did I worry about *how* I was going to accomplish my dream. Which brings me to the **third key principle**: *How* is not important. The unknown can be a major issue for us since we are often so hung up on playing it safe. And because we cannot see the entire way ahead, we instantly give up – telling ourselves that "this dream is impossible." Most times, you will not know *how* or be able to see the way. Act anyway. Do something. Anything. I did not know how I was going to attend St. Joseph's

Academy but a month shy of my twelfth birthday, I enrolled – somehow my parents found the money – and I did, in fact, achieve everything I set out to accomplish at that particular school.

Subsequent Desires

I have utilized the same process in achieving diverse desires such as becoming the top soccer player in my country, as well as coming up with financing to enter the real estate investment field. Remember in Chapter 8 when I described my epic fail in that April 1994 game? Since then, in advance of each soccer game, I would play it over and over in my head and envision the outcome. Obviously, the game ended in my team's favour, as I was not about to envision losing. By the way, who does that? Each time, I saw myself stopping all the shots coming towards my goal net – yes, I played in goal – and I even heard the roar of the crowd as I performed masterfully.

Regarding obtaining financing for real estate investment, I saw myself owning quite a few properties at some of the best locations throughout the city. I saw the proceeds from the rent being deposited in my bank account. I imagined having great tenants who I would treat as valuable customers.

Powerful Insight

You will only do something that you believe you can do. Let me say that again! You will only do something that you believe you can do!! I really, really want you to grasp this fact. To put it another way, you will never attain what you cannot see yourself doing. For instance, I will never become a world champion bungee jumper because I cannot ever see myself doing that.

So – again – significant life success hack: You create your lot in life based on your thoughts and beliefs. Which means that you, and you alone, are solely responsible for the current state of your life. If your life is crappy, it simply means that your thoughts are crappy. Your life is a mirror image of your thoughts. Don't believe me? Let's consult an expert. James Allen said that, "You are today where your thoughts have brought you and you will be tomorrow where your thoughts take you."

Putting in the Work

Now, you might have heard about this thing called the Law of Attraction. I think it would be better called the Law of Action. Thinking positively about your goals and dreams are important, and you also need to act on them. You need to put in the work. Some of us believe we will achieve our goals and dreams by just sitting in a trance while wishing for things to fall in our laps. The truth is that sitting on your ass only brings about more sitting on your ass. You need to get up off your ass and start working towards your goals with faith, trust, belief and focused intent.

Action Exercise

Think about your goals and dreams. Now take the next step toward their accomplishment. It is right in front of you.

Our lives are simply the reflection of our predominant thoughts, our mental attitude.

~ Charles F. Haanel

Chapter 14

Detachment: Paradox of Paradoxes

By surrendering, you obtain your maximum power in all areas.

~ Andy Shaw

IT IS POSSIBLE that this chapter will be a struggle for you, since we are programmed into believing that happiness depends on external things. We become so emotionally attached to events, things and people, that we can forget to focus and work on our goals and dreams.

Where is Derian going with this? What does being detached have to do with taking action on my goals and dreams? Yes, I know this concept of Detachment sounds counter-productive to goal-setting and goal-getting, so please allow me to elaborate. Be honest, are you one of those individuals who likes to *force* things? If so, here's the kicker: Forcing things may lead to you becoming frustrated and concluding that nothing is working for you in the pursuit of your goals. This problem can be solved through Detachment.

What Does Detachment Mean?

Detachment means complete surrender. It means freeing yourself from emotional struggle and anguish. You are still required to take action towards your dreams and desires. Sorry, you are not getting off the hook that easily. However, things work in your favour when you quit forcing the issue. Do not confuse tenacity and determination with forcing.

Trickle-Down Effect

If you refuse to emotionally surrender, you are essentially displaying your lack of trust in the Universe's ability to reward you for your hard work. And here's the trickle-down effect. Without trust, faith becomes lacking. Without faith, you allow doubt to creep in. By fostering an environment of doubt, then fear and its partner, worry, take centre stage. By this point, you might as well kiss your dreams and desires goodbye, as you cannot achieve anything worthwhile if you are doubtful, fearful and worried. Got it?

There's more! Chances are that you will try to control the situation with your own limiting beliefs and patterns of thinking. And when you are hell-bent on controlling things, you are not in acceptance or allowance mode. Without accepting and allowing things to be as they are, you close yourself off from receiving what it is that you truly desire. (Refer to Chapter 5.)

How Letting Go Worked for Me

I know what I just mentioned sounds bizarre, but here is an example that will crystallize this concept of Detachment for you. This particular story is very dear to my heart. About a year after my daughter was born, her mom and I separated. Okay, that was putting it nicely. The truth is that she ended the relationship and told me that she did not want me in her life ever again. While this was tough to accept, what was even more hurtful and heartbreaking was that she informed me that I would never see our daughter again. To justify her actions, I was accused of not being a good father, as well as a host of other things. By the way – as a side note – I forgave her immediately, as by that time, I knew the power of forgiveness. (See Chapter 7.) And, to be fair to her, she eventually apologized nearly 18 years later.

Now back to the story. Over the ensuing years after the separation, it came to my attention that our daughter was living under unsatisfactory conditions. At that point, I made a request to have our daughter reside with me, as I was in a better position to provide a stable environment and lifestyle for her – from both an emotional and financial perspective. However, her mom would have none of it and things became progressively worse for our daughter. As her environment became more and more turbulent, I made repeated requests to her mom, and each time my efforts proved futile.

After more than a decade – 14 years to be exact, but who's counting? – of holding in my heart this vision of our daughter residing with me, I decided to let it go. I had done all I could do. So, I surrendered. I stopped forcing the issue. I decided to trust that things would work out for the best good for both me and my daughter – no matter what the outcome would be. To make a long story short, a month (yes, a month) after deciding to surrender, I received a phone call from my daughter telling me the news that she was pregnant. Given her circumstances, in which no one was willing to accommodate her and her future baby, the stage was set for her to reside with me.

Paradox of Paradoxes

Was it a coincidence that the moment I detached myself from wanting my daughter to reside with me, the event took place in quick order? I think not. And did surrendering mean that I no longer cared about my desire to have my daughter reside with me? No! Not at all. You see, Detachment does not mean that you stop caring about, or quit working toward your goals and dreams. Nor is it about denying the joys of achievement. Here's the process in a nutshell: You have identified your goal. You have done – or are currently doing – all you can. In other words, you took – or are taking – action. Finally, you simply let go of an attachment to any particular outcome. And, if what you are working on is the right thing for you at that particular period in your life, guess what, you will have it. If it is not the right time for you to have it, or if it is not even the correct thing for you to have, then something better will show up in its place. So, in actuality, there's never a need to stress or worry about anything. Just put in the work and the rest will take care of itself. Neither people, things nor events will be able to deter you. Full stop!

Ok! So, let us take the example I provided earlier. I had a goal – having my daughter reside with me. I repeatedly took action (yes, I am purposely making sure Taking Action stays at the forefront of your brain) to bring about this desire – trying to get her mom's approval through a series of discussions (too many if you asked me). I eventually *surrendered* whereby I got to the point of acceptance that if my daughter resided with me, then great. However, if not, then that would be fine too. In other words, I made the decision to be okay with either outcome. And not only did it turn out great, my granddaughter came as part of the package. How freaking awesome is that?

What are you attached to?

This is a good time to take a look at some of the things from which you need to detach yourself. The first is attachment to another person or to other people. There is a tendency to believe that the labour required to achieve our goals and dreams is someone else's responsibility. You want someone to *do it* for you. No. No. No. That is for you to do. Others will come along to assist, but your job is not to become dependent on them. Do not be a parasite.

You may be living vicariously through others, most often through your children. Stop it! Get some goals for yourself. I love my daughter wholeheartedly. However, I have no attachment to the decisions she makes. In other words, I do not view her lifestyle as a reflection of me as a parent. She has to live her own life and follow her own path. I care about her to the extent that I let her grow without my meddling.

Please note: There are boundaries in regards to discipline and parental guidance and there are guidelines, however, I do not get caught up in having expectations of her. If she needs guidance, I gladly oblige. However, as she is getting older, I only provide guidance as requested. If you disagree with my method of parenting, oh well. I do not see the need to offer any justification or to defend myself. I have detached myself from these behaviours as well.

Which brings us back around to being attached to seeking approval from others. (Refer to Chapter 11.) By now I bet you are no longer engaging in this practice because you are on a roll and getting your act together.

Being Right

How about attachment to being right? This was my Achilles Heel. I got so caught up in being right that every discussion turned into a debate, and I learned nothing in the process because I was too busy yapping away. Thankfully, my desire to chase my dreams to become the best person I can be, steered me away from this very bad habit of needing to be right all the time. While I can still engage in a good verbal challenge, I am now able to focus on what really matters: taking strides toward my goals and dreams.

Action Exercise

LET GO.

Plain and simple.

Just S.U.R.R.E.N.D.E.R.!

Do your best and leave the rest.

Don't get too caught up with the outcome.

~ Derian B. Tuitt

Call to Action

HAVE YOU BEEN sitting around and fantasizing about living the life you desire? And if so, how much longer are you willing to continue procrastinating before taking any action? One month? A year? A decade? Take a quick moment to calculate the number of opportunities you have missed out on so far as a result of not taking action.

Now, in this book you have been presented with life success hacks. Would you agree that they have jolted and inspired you to get moving and take action? Why be sick and tired of not feeling fulfilled, when, by deciding to take these simple actions, you will be living a life of purpose and clear intention right away? This moment is where the rubber meets the road. Now is the time for you to decide that you can and will achieve everything you've always imagined. My One-Year Exit Strategy (O-YES) program is your launching pad. With this program you will learn:

- How to move from a life of mediocrity and tedium to one of passion and fulfillment

- How to discover your true gift – what you were placed on Earth to do and be, rather than doing what simply pays the bills

- How to recognize your best timing to leave your unfulfilling job and reclaim your freedom to thrive

- How to trust in the flow of money in your life

Here is what you can do, immediately: Write on your calendar or in your day book on today's date that this is the day you are contacting Derian Tuitt. Then, call me or send a text to 613-291-4684 or email me at derian@deriantuitt.com and let me know you are ready to schedule your 15-minute free consultation session. Take action now. The people who live life to the fullest are those who take action regarding their goals and dreams. Stop settling for mediocrity. Instead of sitting around wishing for success to fall in your lap, your challenge is to start playing the game of life on a whole new level and become the greatest version of yourself. Ready? Now is the time to contact me. Let's get started.

Acknowledgements

THANKS TO HUBERT RAYNE for insisting that I bring this book to the market. Your belief in me is remarkable. You are a great mentor and friend. Thanks to everyone at Celebrity Expert Author Publishing for your insight and creativity. Thank you, Lynn Thompson, creator of The Living on Purpose Playgram. You did an impeccable job of editing and polishing this book. The many hours we spent together were fulfilling.

Most importantly, thank you Debrina. You have been the source of my inspiration from the moment I laid eyes on you. A big thank you also for giving me the greatest gift ever – My Dearest, Ms. Nadia.